What Do We Tell the

CHILDREN?

What Do We Tell the CHILDREN?

Talking to Kids about Death and Dying

Joseph M. Primo

Abingdon Press
Nashville

WHAT DO WE TELL THE CHILDREN?
TALKING TO KIDS ABOUT DEATH AND DYING

Copyright © 2013 by Abingdon Press

All rights reserved.

This book is printed on acid-free paper.

Library of Congress Cataloging-in-Publication Data

Primo, Joseph M.
What do we tell the children? : talking to kids about death and dying / by Joseph M. Primo.
pages cm
ISBN 978-1-4267-6049-5 (binding; adhesive; soft black : alk. paper) 1. Children and death. 2. Terminally ill parents. 3. Families of the terminally ill—Services for. 4. Bereavement in children. 5. Church work with the bereaved. 6. Church work with children. I. Title.
BF723.D3P75 2013
259'.6082—dc23

2013023277

Disclaimer: All names and significant details have been changed by the author to protect the identity of clients.

13 14 15 16 17 18 19 20 21 22—10 9 8 7 6 5 4 3 2 1
MANUFACTURED IN THE UNITED STATES OF AMERICA

For Jeanette, my parents and grandparents, Sid, Anne,

and the extraordinary children of Good Grief

Contents

Acknowledgments

This work is not accomplished in isolation but in community. My colleagues are remarkable people, and they influence my life in so many ways. I am particularly grateful for my staff. I would be lost without them. I am grateful for all my Good Grief colleagues, the Board of Directors, and especially Good Grief facilitators, whose commitment to Good Grief is like no other.

My colleagues and friends at the National Alliance for Grieving Children are true champions for children and families throughout the country. Every day of their lives they tirelessly advocate for children, and their commitment to the cause is most admirable. I am thankful for each of them and the humor, integrity, and joy they bring to every conversation.

I am grateful for my old friends at the Connecticut Hospice, especially Lou Gonzalez, Rev. Charles Woody, and Dr. Scott Long. The entire staff shaped me at a time when death's presence was so palpable, and at times overwhelming, that I thought I might not make it to thirty. Many thanks to Lenore and Harry, whose last words are a daily reminder.

Many mentors and dear friends supported me over this past decade as I immersed myself in death and dying. Although their love for the topic may have been less than mine, their support of me never wavered: Andrew Nurkin, Kristyn Primo, Dianne Bilyak, Jacqueline Richard, Anne Corron, Barbara Walker, Dr. Ann Blankenship, Dr. Donna Rica, Dr. Margaret Farley, Fr. Jaime Lara, Dr. Kristen Leslie, Dr. Herbert Anderson, and all my pals at Yale Divinity School.

When people ask me if my work is depressing, I tell them that it is filled with fun and authenticity. But every day I walk by Good Grief's Wall of Remembrance, on which children have tacked images of loved ones who have died. The wall is the worst part of my day. The people in those photos do not experience what I witness: brokenness, struggle, healing, love, rebuilding, and the extraordinary character of their children, oftentimes brought out because of death. I am most saddened for the deceased, and I carry their stories with me. The children and families of Good Grief inspire me each and every day. To witness their growth and grief work is an honor. Many thanks to my Kingda Ka buddies. I'll remember forever that day and the courage I saw in you. Lastly, some of the stories in this book might sound like yours. In this book I retell stories that are universal in their nature. The details of each story are how I imagine them or remember their retelling, as I was not there when death appeared. All names and details have been changed to protect each family's privacy.

Good Grief kids are my favorite teachers. I think you will understand why well before you finish reading this book.

For Additional Support and Resources Please Visit:

Good Grief

    www.good-grief.org

The National Alliance for Grieving Children

    www.childrengrieve.org

What Do We Tell The Children?

    www.howkidsgrieve.com

Prologue

"Be not afraid" were the first words Pope John Paul II spoke when he stood at a window overlooking a massive crowd only moments after his election by the College of Cardinals. I first heard these words in 1996 in a video about the papacy, a discounted film I made my parents purchase for me. As a religiously fanatic teen, I thought the pope had a far cooler job than the president and I didn't understand why all my peers talked about becoming president when, according to Catholic law, any baptized Catholic male could grow up to be the pope.

Bill Clinton did not wear snazzy robes or drive in a white popemobile. In my mind, being a world religious leader for an indefinite amount of time totally surpassed the powers of the presidency. Oh, and believers kiss the pope's ring. That is the epitome of an instant ego boost. You don't get that in the White House!

While fantasizing about how I would run my papacy, I was hardly aware that those first scriptural words that the newly elected pope spoke would become a mantra for me a few months later when I witnessed my aunt drop dead at the kitchen table.

I was raised Catholic in an Irish-Italian household. Every stereotype about Irish-Italian Catholics applies to me—every single one. For example, my great-grandfather emigrated from Sciacca, Sicily, and brought with him the Feast of Madonna del Soccorso. For the past century, as a result of my great-grandfather and his friends, Bostonians have processed a large statue of the Virgin Mary through the North End of Boston during a three-day religious party called the Fisherman's Feast.

My people, these feisty Italians, strap an eight-year-old girl to a crane, dress her like an angel, and swing her from a balcony as they toss confetti, pray in Italian, and rile up the crowd. I attended this feast every August until I was an adult. The only year I missed was 1996.

That summer I missed the Fisherman's Feast because of an invitation from my Irish grandparents, who encouraged my sister and me to spend a week with them. I loved spending time at their home in Maine. It was a fairly secluded house in the woods. My grandfather knew the dirtiest jokes, which he would share with me when we went fishing. It was the only time I got to hear those jokes, because my grandmother was not around to yell at him for telling them. Our fishing trips captured the quintessential nature of our grandfather-grandson relationship. My grandmother, however, admittedly wished she had become a nun and was determined to make me a priest. When Gramps and I finished fishing and telling jokes, I would return home, where Grandma was waiting. She and I would pray, which naturally made me feel less guilty about all the dirty jokes.

This back-and-forth game of baiting the hook, telling a joke, and repenting in prayer went on for a few days, until my aunts and uncles arrived. They drove up from Massachusetts in time for lunch. My sister and I were thrilled because we knew the adults would spoil us. We also loved the stories they shared about their youth. I suppose it made them more relatable. And, of course, their fake Irish brogue somehow made them great storytellers.

This lunch quickly became an unforgettable moment in my life. Once everyone arrived we got down to business. Tuna melts were made. The fruit salad was tossed, and we debated whether to eat pie then or save it for dinner.

The adults sat around the table eating their lunch and complaining about the increase in toll rates on the turnpike. My sister and I sat at the counter, eavesdropping and plotting how we could get pie for lunch and dinner.

Not long after we sat down to eat, we were startled by a frantic scream. My Aunt Barbara looked on in horror as my Aunt Jeanette slouched over the table.

There are only a few moments in my life that I remember with such painful clarity. This is probably the clearest.

Within moments of Barbara's yelp, chairs were flung across the room, the table was pushed against the wall, and my grandmother and uncle were lowering Jeanette to the floor to begin resuscitating her. They would remain in that position, in chase of her fleeting life, for the next forty-five minutes. My Uncle Charlie, Jeanette's husband, was responsible for chest compressions as my grandmother counted and pushed breath into Jeanette's lungs.

My sister Kristyn and I stood there. We just stood there watching Jeanette's color change and the faces of the adults turn to unforgiving fear.

My grandfather was a stoic man, but he fumbled with each word as he spoke with the 911 operator. He couldn't tie his shoelaces as he prepared to go to the hospital. Kristyn and I stared at the unfolding scene until I decided I had to do something. Pushing my way through the adults with Kristyn in tow, I grabbed my grandmother's rosaries to prepare for some fierce praying. I looked at Kristyn and saw her distress.

What was I supposed to do with my little sister? I paused, looked around my grandparents' bedroom where I had rushed to get the rosaries, and noticed that the closet had a lock. Tossing my sister into the closet, I shouted, "Be not afraid!" and locked her in. Running out of the room, I kept shouting, "Be not afraid!" I was trying to convince her that it was OK; but I was also trying to convince myself as my chest pounded harder and harder and as I stood in the corner crying while I prayed—prayed and watched my grandmother count to ten and breathe into Jeanette.

Forty-five minutes after CPR began, the volunteer EMTs arrived. Charlie and my grandmother stepped back from Jeanette. Their work was done. Some device was hooked up to Jeanette, and I was shooed from the room. From around the corner, I heard the device's robotic voice counting and instructing. I listened to the whimpers of the adults and shouted up the stairwell to my sister, "Be not afraid! I said, 'Be not afraid!'" I could hear the crowds, like those gathered for the election of John Paul II in Saint Peter's Square, cheering and shouting, "Good advice, boy. Good advice!"

Jeanette was loaded onto a stretcher and ushered down the lawn to the ambulance. The ambulance sat in the driveway for another ten minutes as the medics attempted to resuscitate her while my grandparents and Charlie waited to follow behind in their car. The tension was growing as the rest of us waited on the stoop. "What are they waiting for?" we asked one another every few minutes. *Drive already!* And then, almost in a demonic voice, I began cursing at the paramedics. I shouted unholy and bad words that my grandfather would use only if the fishhook caught his finger or the big bass got away. No one stopped me. My fear turned to rage, and so too did the grief that followed in the days and months ahead.

"Be not afraid." All these years later it is still an expression I say to myself often in tense situations. When I was a hospice chaplain, I frequently walked into rooms that contained sobbing family members or a terrified patient. "Be not afraid," I'd tell myself.

Now as a director of two children's bereavement centers, when a dad calls me to ask how he should tell his three- and seven-year-old children that Mom died this morning, I still tell myself, "Be not afraid." Fear is usually present in my work, and each time I experience it I come to better understand why I felt so alone and isolated after Jeanette died. It's easy to look away but a lot harder to reach out and touch the flame.

I started high school two weeks after Jeanette's death. The experience of going to high school was scary enough, but now my mind was clogged with images of my dead aunt. What had I witnessed? What is this thing we call death? How was she hugging me at 1:00 p.m. and dead by 1:30? Where did she go, and how do I make sense of what I saw? And, how about those prayers I so frantically prayed? No saint could have prayed like me on that day!

I wanted to talk about it. I needed to talk about it. In the days leading up to Jeanette's funeral my family had entertained some discussion of that August afternoon. But by the time school started in September, I was alone. My sister was afraid to talk about it, most likely because she did not want to end up in a closet again. My grandparents were in Maine, and we all knew that my grandmother was struggling with what happened, so I didn't want to trouble her with my grief.

I wrote about my feelings in typing class, a skill-development class that students were required to take freshman year. Every opportunity I had, once a week for four months, I manipulated the assignment to meet my needs. If the assignment was to write about nature, I would write about the cycle of life and death, and retell the story of Jeanette's death. If the week's topic was sports, I'd talk about the game of life and death, winners and losers.

One day in January the teacher asked me about it. She said, "You type fast and you're a good writer." I proudly told her, "Everything I write is true." Instantly, she put the narrative together. Her eyes bulged, which was quite noticeable given her small stature. "Oh, well, this is just inappropriate. I don't want to see anymore of this. No more!" she barked at me as if I had done something wrong. She didn't even take a second to ask a follow-up question or to pause before responding. And in a millisecond that was the end of that. I was ashamed and felt like I should apologize for upsetting her. The only outlet I knew was gone. I didn't have a computer at home. It didn't occur to me to get a journal, nor would I have felt safe writing in a journal, because I didn't want to chance my parents reading what I was feeling. So I held it all in.

Years later I found myself at Yale Divinity School studying end-of-life counseling and medical ethics. By this time, Jeannette's death was something I talked about from time to time if the conversation permitted, but it was not often. I suppose, in search for meaning, I had landed in a place where I could further explore that event and its impact on me. It was not until I became a hospice chaplain, watched many people die, and found myself supporting children that I realized the impact of Jeanette's death and our societal dilemma. In pursuit of raising awareness and empowering communities to choose a different way to help grieving children, I wrote this book; and I did so with the hundreds of grieving children who have shaped my understanding. I also did so with my fourteen-year-old self in mind.

By the time April 1997 rolled around, I was flunking math and other subjects. I could not concentrate because images of Jeanette and fear of my mortality kept popping to mind, unprovoked and uninvited. Soon my grief became physical. I developed chronic belly-aches and a fear that my whole family would soon be dead. The year after Jeanette's death was a giant burp in my life simply because no one would openly talk about her death, what I witnessed, or my grief. No one even simply asked me how I was doing.

If only I knew to shout at all the adults: *"Be not afraid. Be not afraid!"*

A Caregiver's Perspective: The Power of Presence

It's midnight and you get the frantic call. You knew it would come but didn't know when. It's Mary, and her son, Tony, is dying. "Can you come?" "Of course, I'm on the way." As you get off the elevator, you spot Tony's younger sister sitting with her grandparents in the waiting area. Death is hard enough, but talking about it with children is even more difficult. What will I say?

The hospice where I was a chaplain was a fifty-four-bed facility. It was the first hospice in the United States and a place where I ministered to more than two thousand people over a four-year period. Most of the patients were middle aged or older adults, but many were young. I could not relate to the parents watching their child die or to the children who watched their parent wither his or her way into the coffin. It was just too far out of my own experience. At first, I thought the way to be helpful was to relate so I could help alleviate the pain. I was not sure what the patients expected from me or how to provide comfort; but I did know that I was the chaplain and that I was expected to provide some sort of support.

Perhaps you are not so inexperienced, but it took me a while to figure out my role. I often just found myself at the bedside. I showed up and waited for the rest to unfold. I realized I could empathize with the pain of watching someone die, and I could feel my own distress from my personal history as I watched someone breathe his or her last breath. From witnessing my aunt die, I had learned about the power of being present, listening, and showing that I care. I learned this because of its absence when I needed it. My experience of isolation, fear, and uncertainty gave me perspective and empathy in some crucial situations. So, I tried out this approach and hoped for the best.

Over time I came to understand the uniqueness of each person's grief and the ways in which a caregiver can be a roadblock or a full-fledged detour in someone's healing. Often, those kindhearted folk who show up to help actually get in the way. They say the wrong things despite the best intentions. At hospice I watched many kind "helpers"—usually neighbors, church ladies, or hovering family members—attempt to be helpful. The result, however, often left patients frustrated and unheard or unaffirmed as they were surrounded by overly positive friends, people who would say, "You're going to beat this," or, "Don't talk that way," despite the patient's obvious and imminent demise. Sometimes these well-meaning people said nothing at all, as if nothing were happening, and that was unhelpful too. And when these same helpers spoke these same kinds of words to children, whether as patients or family, the kids were effectively told not to feel their feelings and think their thoughts. They were told, and they heard correctly, that they were wrong: *Think this way, not that;* or even, *Don't ask too many questions.*

I was tested on numerous occasions. I would be with a patient or family and hear their story. They would say or do something and I'd respond by thinking: *Tell your mother you love her. Oh, forgive and let go already.* Judgments and feelings were constantly present.

I thought I could manage other people's lives and pain better than they could for themselves. Navigating my way through my own ideas and judgments was no small task, but I quickly learned the power of caring presence and letting things be what they were going to be (and perhaps needed to be). I began to realize that I could not take away someone's pain, and my job was not to make it better. But arriving at this conclusion was a process, and at times it was labored at best.

There was so much death and so much suffering during this time in my life, as I watched so many people die. Although some days were overwhelming with sadness, others were packed with laughter and joy. I witnessed some of the most beautiful good-byes and final moments one could imagine. Yet, the sad parts, either because of my personality or their prevalence, seemed to stick out more. My work as a caregiver had all the elements for a crisis of faith and purpose as I sorted through the stories and went to work every day. Like you, I wanted to be a good caregiver more than anything, but the harder I tried, the quicker I found myself doubting everything. How do you measure impact? Love? Compassion? Making a difference? The analytical skills I developed during my academic studies did not help me understand these questions or the fatigue that accompanied witnessing people die every day.

As I wrestled with these questions and their implications on how I understood my purpose at the bedside, I approached my supervisor and suggested a title change. At first he wasn't sure if I was asking for a promotion or a demotion. OK, so who goes to his or her boss and suggests that he rework the entire traditional model for pastoral care because the shoes don't fit? I did. I was convinced that the problem was external, some variable other than me. I tried to help him understand why every time I introduced myself as the chaplain or someone looked at my name badge I felt out of sorts. "Is that what I am, and is that really how they see me?" I asked him. "I don't know what I am doing. Maybe 'Chaplain' isn't the right title for me," I told my supervisor. "Could we call me a spiritual counselor or something?" My experience, my shifting of expectations, and my realization that I could not take away someone's pain, knocked me off my footing. I thought, *If I can't fix it or make it better, then what's the point? What am I doing here?*

I feel a little embarrassed when I look back on those conversations, but I understand that I felt a degree of desperation as I tried to comprehend my role as a caregiver. Because all my preconceived ideas about what it means to "help" someone had been challenged and proved ineffective, I assumed the problem lay elsewhere. I felt powerless and unsure of everything. Perhaps this is a caregiver's rock bottom, because soon thereafter I understood that the problem lay with me, my expectations, and what I believed helping and supporting someone meant.

My need to reshape how I saw myself as a caregiver provided me with a deeper understanding of how I could be more effective, but it also helped me understand better what suffering is and our collective need for compassionate people who can listen and be present. This process started me in the direction of becoming a caring presence, a witness, and a companion to those in need of support, rather than a "fixer" or someone who could help resolve grief.

Now when I experience doubt about my effectiveness, I think it is inherently good and serves a deep and meaningful purpose to my work and what motivates me to show up every day. I see it as an opportunity to pause, reflect, and reassess.

The first time I truly had to pause, reflect, and reassess my motivations was when a thirty-four-year-old mom with nine- and eleven-year-old sons was dying of a brain tumor at hospice. She had just opened an Italian bakery when she was first diagnosed. Leslie reminded me of the loud Italian women in the bakeries of Boston who always encouraged me to eat more cannolis than my mother thought was permissible. Leslie's dream of becoming a shop owner had been fulfilled only a few months before meeting me. Now, she lay in a bed, her head distortedly oval-shaped, a cranium put back together after a tumor scavenger hunt. Leslie had come to hospice knowing she was there to die, which isn't necessarily an obvious supposition to most newly admitted patients who are transitioning from a fighter's mentality to surrendering to the reality of their approaching death.

In Leslie's last days I often found her boys sitting by the window, disengaged from their mom. She wasn't the same mom anymore. Her personality had quickly become unrecognizable as the tumor pressed on her frontal lobe. On the day she died I did what I had done for her a dozen times before: I pushed an electric piano up to her bedside and played Frank Sinatra tunes.

A few weeks prior, she had come to the weekly church service, where I played the piano. Afterward, she approached me and asked if I could play any songs other than those "Jesus tunes." When I replied, "Sinatra," she requested a show at noon and waddled her way back to her room to prep for my arrival. There, she put on lipstick, a sparkling blouse, and a shimmering head scarf. She was painting her fingernails when I arrived with the keyboard at my side. She was ready for a show.

When Leslie died I was sick to my stomach but unsure of what to do with the complexity of emotions I, "the professional," was feeling. I wondered, *Am I allowed to feel or should I be more distant?* I'm not sure if I was sad for her boys, sad on account of her premature dying, or sad because her story was an all-too-common tragedy.

That night I invited Dianne, a colleague from divinity school, to visit me. I lived on the third floor of a late-nineteenth-century home, and as I approached the last steps and saw Dianne's face through the glass door, I dropped. I plunged to my knees, skipping the last few steps, and wept. I felt safe and could finally let out my grief, all those feelings I had held in as I had helped Leslie's family say good-bye. And on the other side of the glass stood Dianne, watching as my sunken head bobbed up and down and my shoulders bounced while the tears flowed.

Moments later I was mortified, convinced that the death business wasn't for me, that God had screwed up on me and on Leslie, making me unworthy of offering another thought or prayer. But then Dianne asked these questions in a corny voice in order to provoke laughter: "Do you not bleed? Are you immune from suffering?" I didn't laugh as she expected. Instead, by letting out the intense feelings I was experiencing, I began to understand the reality and depths of the work of death and dying. I was starting to understand better the ministry I offered. I began to appreciate the work and my role in a new way. I began to see another way of helping. It was the first moment at which I fully understood that being present, witnessing someone's pain and companioning him or her through it, offering empathy and love, and not judging the person was making a difference.

I like to think that my willingness to be honest and vulnerable with myself and to reflect on my experiences with death and grief has informed my work and provided me with the ability to appreciate the situation differently each time. I like to think that each of these experiences prepared me for my next encounter while also helping me be more responsive and attuned to those seeking care.

As someone fulfilling a spiritual need, I naturally saw my work at hospice as spiritual. But, I think anything to do with dying, death, and bereavement is spiritual work no matter how one approaches it. Ministry to the dying and grieving forces us to see, truly see, our own mortality; and from that seeing we are challenged to make meaning out of our own lives. Although everyone else may be able to go on ignoring death's constant presence, caregivers are keenly aware that each of us has a day to die. I think that knowledge makes working with the dying and bereaved a series of spiritual encounters. Our work begs us to ask, perhaps over and over again, how we fit into a world that is filled with grief, despite our society's inability to engage and cope with this universal truth.

Finding one's comfort in a world filled with grief requires a form of mindfulness or attunement, which I will discuss later. A caregiver's sense of connection with the bereaved, and a developed comfort with simply being present, is crucial. The grief experience often taunts a person's spiritual stability, flusters one's sense of self, and throws into question one's purpose in the world. At the core of the grief experience, ironically, emotional healing happens because of this flustered, spiritual process. It is accompanied by many feelings, some of which are complex and hard to describe; but this process also leads us toward finding a reason to continue living and a purpose for rebuilding our lives.

Whether we are experiencing the grief or witnessing it, bereavement is a spiritual act, an emotional and intellectual discernment that tries to process and understand suffering and the challenging truths that often accompany it. Grief is complex and has many layers. The cause of a person's death, the people involved, the question of why wonderful people die, and all the accompanying details influence how we perceive a person's death.

For example, some deaths feel unjust. I think it is safe to say that when a thirty-three-year-old father of three dies of an aneurysm while his fourth baby is on her way, it feels unfair and unjust to most of us. Most people will agree that the narrative does not add up; something is inherently flawed about that man's demise. It feels like it should not have happened. The work of his widow and child, friends and parents, is spiritual work. How do they make sense of that tragedy? Where was God? What was God thinking? Why do humans experience suffering no matter the quality of their character?

These are some profound questions, and they are at the core of many bereaved people's stories and meaning making, no matter if the person is six or sixty. When I experienced grief as a teen, these were things that I wanted to know. How? Why? Was God punishing us or tying to tell us something? In my fourteen-year-old mind, I believed there were clear-cut answers and perhaps a prescribed way to understand my grief better. It sent me in quest of meaning, in search of understanding other people's lives and deaths and coming to terms with a fragile and quite uncertain existence.

At hospice, I witnessed many people wrestle with these basic, simple, but oh-so-complex questions in an effort to explain suffering, especially when it was their first and deepest encounter with such raw pain. Each effort and every attempt to understand suffering has a purpose, even if understanding finally eludes us. Attempting to understand pain and suffering shapes how we see the world and how we explain death to our children. This process and the dialogue we have with ourselves and others, however, are fairly individualized. Although we pick up plenty of cues from our religious, cultural, and societal heritage, we best understand suffering through the lens of our individual experiences, our own personal grief story.

I do not mean to assume or imply that all grief is suffering or that suffering is always a characteristic of grief. Surprisingly, it's not. I once walked to the bedside of a dying young woman and found her husband crying at her side. It appeared to be profound pain, a devastating loss. They were young. He looked distraught; she appeared healthy, so I assumed the diagnosis and her impending death had happened overnight. I approached him timidly, uncertain of what he would say or what I could expect from him. Pulling up a chair, I sat down next to him and waited. I suppose I could have introduced myself, asked his name, or said something meaningless like, "She appears comfortable." Instead I chose silence and caring presence.

When the soon-to-be widower looked up, he said, "I am so grateful for our lives together, and I'm glad she will be gone soon. She doesn't need to fight for me. I just want her pain to be over. This terrible breast cancer robbed her of everything." His tears continued to drip from his chin, now jutting over the handrails of the bed, to her pillow.

I saw those tears in a new way, something I could not have imagined on my own when I stood in the doorway making assumptions about the situation. My hesitation, the reverence I had when approaching that patient's space, allowed me to be present rather than fill the room with words that had no context, no meaning, no purpose other than my own grasping for direction, as I entered the unknown space that was this woman's death and her husband's good-bye.

There is so much uncertainty surrounding death and grief. We don't know from where it will come, how it will go, and if the end is really the end. Often, we are unsure whether the dying woman knows she is dying. Will she admit it to us? Has she admitted it to herself? Should we send a card? Should it say "Get well" or "See you on the other side"? Should we talk about the child's dead mom or will that upset him? The uncertainty around death and grief, and our lack of vocabulary to talk about it, often leaves us crippled.

We say meaningless things because we do not know what to say. We ignore the grieving because we don't know what to do with these people and how to fit them into our daily living as they regroup and rebuild their lives or prepare to die.

The mystery of death and our language around it, both in its coming and its going, play a vital role in culture, faith, and our future. I am of the mind-set that previously prescribed religious or societal beliefs should not wholly define the mystery of death and each person's unique experience of it. I hope this will become clear as we explore the complexities of grief and the need for unrestrained exploration, especially for children who are seeking facts. I also hope that the need for taking risks, as our society redefines—or rather, begins to define—our traditions and language around death, becomes clear and that we find the courage to let our language evolve. The risks I propose are simple, courageous acts of mindfulness and caring presence. The demand for competent adults who are able and willing to be present with grieving children is great, and the first step in getting there is to take a good look at ourselves.

Put On Your Own Oxygen Mask First

B efore we can proceed to talk about children and their grief, we need to know our own grief story. Our interactions with grieving children, our presence and responses, are skewed by many variables: our age, previous losses, religious beliefs, cultural heritage, and, of course, our profession and social role. It is important to understand these prejudices because they will influence our expectations of how a child should grieve or what a child's grief looks like. This is true for each of us, and unless we are willing to dive into our own grief experience and reflect on our grief story, we will not be able to identify those feelings and discomforts that affect our perception of other people's stories. Through our own careful examination of our fears, preconceived beliefs, deaths, disenfranchised grief, and the ways in which each of us achieves emotional safety through ideas that can become rigid beliefs that are not applicable to everyone, we are able to better support the bereaved, especially children.

When I train facilitators of children's support groups, I never start the training with children's grief, even though that's the subject the facilitators have signed up to learn about. We never dive right into childhood development or what grief looks like for a kid. Instead, I dress up like a flight attendant and take out a mock oxygen mask. "When this thing spirals, folks, you've got to put on your oxygen mask first. Then you can help the child next to you." Well, that makes sense to everyone. We all need to breathe, and it's better for us to prepare ourselves first so that we can help the children. So, many thanks to whoever came up with that life-saving advice, because that same teaching is crucial for successfully helping adults and kids with their grief.

On the first day of training I have everyone create a loss line. It is a simple task that is full of emotion, memories, and sharing. No matter how creative someone is (or is not), each trainee sits down with a large poster board and maps out his or her grief story. The trainees make collages that map, from birth to the present moment, dreams that never came to fruition, loves that fizzled, parents who died, unwelcome moves across states that left friends behind, the deaths of pets and friends, job losses, and all sorts of other things that are a part of life. If you have never done this exercise, take some time and do it now. Create your own loss line. What memories are stirred? Are there any patterns? What other important life events followed?

This exercise exemplifies our grief story. Reflecting on life, seeing the years that were full of grief or hope, and returning to memories that time has since silenced, the trainees build on their empathy and can more clearly see the ways in which their story might lead to judgments and assumptions that would make them less effective with others. I call this grief work. And doing grief work leads to grief knowledge.

Grief work is so important because, for the most part, we've forgotten how to do it. We no longer have transference of grief knowledge from our elders to the next generation. The knowledge has been lost because a discomfort with grief and a denial of our mortality have silenced our stories. Our lack of socially prescribed ways of dealing with death as a community directly affects each of us, especially our children. Kids look to adults in order to learn, acquire knowledge and facts, and better understand life. When a grieving child—or any child for that matter—looks to an adult to gain a better understanding of death but no one is able to provide honest or clear responses, it is unsettling for the child.

I believe our ability to honestly engage our mortality and grief has shifted dramatically in the last 150 years from an intimate familiarity to a disconnect and discomfort with death. Both our expectations and rituals have changed. Up until the twentieth century we were a primarily agricultural society in which children and adults were routinely interacting with nature and the cycle of life, watching animals give birth as well as die. It was a day and time when the sick were cared for at home and the death of both the young and the old seemed like an ordinary, albeit often unwelcome, part of life. Although medical science offers many blessings, it has also led us to create new expectations about death. Nowadays, we like to think that death is specifically for people over ninety or one hundred. We are OK with them dying. That seems natural to us. They lived a long life. We may miss them, but we are not surprised by their deaths.

In large part, this shift in attitude and experience can be attributed to medical advancements, but it also has something to do with the rapid change of our death rituals. Rituals are a crucial characteristic of how adults and children alike understand and comprehend death. The American Civil War, for example, drastically changed our death rituals and our vocabulary for talking about grief.

During that war, Confederate and Union soldiers were embalmed and brought home for burial. This was a new practice, in which families could now expect their dead to be returned to them and buried in their family plot. Eventually, President Abraham Lincoln underwent the same procedure after his assassination. Everyone was so impressed that the new embalming practices allowed the president to be transported across the country. As a result, the practice's popularity increased, first among the rich and then among the masses. In a short period of time this led to the creation of "stand alone" funeral parlors, which replaced the parlor in the family home. No longer did the family care for their deceased; now strangers were responsible for the disposition of the dead for a fee, creating a new economy with its own ideas, agendas, and practices.

Funeral homes erased the smell and look of death. The dead looked lifelike and asleep, in what the funeral industry now calls a "memory photo." That's where a huge shift in our culture began. We transitioned from death to "a sleeping appearance." Our comfort and intimacy with death continues to be foreign. Funeral homes are staged to keep death tidy and to force us to control our emotions as lines form at the casket and the bereaved shake the hands of all those "paying their respects." The dead are made to look like the living, and this disguise affects our understanding of death.

Think about this. If you spend a Saturday afternoon watching a cooking channel on television, as I often do, you'll hear the chef say, "We eat with our eyes." He will then go on to talk about our senses and how our eyes, taste buds, and brains work together to create the entire, magical flavor in our mouths. Our eyes help us understand. They communicate with our brain. Our current funeral rituals have removed our ability to touch and interact with the dead and see them as they naturally are. Our senses aren't sending honest messages to our brains and aiding us in our understanding of death.

I believe that our lack of interaction with the dead—death's place as a taboo in our society—has affected our ability to talk openly about death and grief. Today, death is something that happens behind closed doors. Children do not often see it in real life, despite the fact that it is all over our television. Children understand dead squirrels on the side of the road, dead fish, and dead dogs. Parents tend to be comfortable with those teachable moments. But what about dead Grandma? Well, that's when the folklore begins, which I will discuss shortly.

I view our mortuary practices, how we handle and deal with our dead, as interconnected with those taboos surrounding death and with our lack of vocabulary to talk about death and grief. The funeral ritual, after all, is an integral part to our good-byes and how we comprehend or process that a person has died.

Depending on the circumstances, anticipatory grief can begin as we first contemplate a loved one's impending death. Grief can also launch into full swing when we learn about the death. It is then exacerbated during the funeral ritual when the living are reunited with the dead at a funeral home and see the dead for the very last time. These experiences can set us on a path, healthy or unhealthy, for our grief work. Our expectations about death and grief and the rituals surrounding them affect our grief work and healing.

Our grief work is an ongoing process that lasts a lifetime as we lose friends, family members, and even parts of ourselves (i.e., our own characteristics of a healthy body). Through this process we can build coping skills and resiliency, preparing us for future grief. We don't have to be victimized or defeated by death.

Our own stories, prejudices, and assumptions can dilute our thoughts and feelings about other people's grief, making it important that we take the time to understand the complexities of our grief and acknowledge our own emotional baggage.

Grief looks different depending on many variables, including culture. Although I advocate for everyone to have the opportunity to express his or her emotions, I am still surprised when I see people completely vulnerable in front of strangers. One morning during the summer of 2004, I was sitting at my desk and looking at Long Island Sound before making my rounds to visit hospice patients. It was a morning ritual, in which I reflected on the lives that had ended in the wee hours of that morning and I thought about the memories and love that would be shared that day. I suppose it gave me perspective on days when I found the institution dysfunctional and I hoped that, despite family dynamics and feuds, there would be a lot of beautiful moments and healing that day.

I got a call from the admission nurse asking for support. A twenty-nine-year-old mother of a two-year-old was en route to the hospice. She was being transferred from Yale-New Haven Hospital, which befuddled the staff since the patient was actively dying in the ambulance. Someone knowing that she has a terminal illness is quite different from someone actively dying. When we are actively dying, we are on our way out. Organs are shutting down, breathing is sporadic, and death is hours or moments away.

I met the patient at the front door. She was wearing an oxygen mask, and her skin was pale and frigid to the touch. Her eyes were fixed on the ceiling, and everything her body was communicating told us that she had only minutes left.

The usual routine for admitting a patient included a lot of paperwork, questions, and the introduction of nurses, doctors, a social worker, and me, the chaplain. This mom, however, went straight to her room, and protocols were tossed aside so that doctors could ensure her comfort.

Shortly after her arrival, her family came to her bedside. Then her friends came; then her neighbors; then the neighborhood. Folk from the church came next, and then came death.

The wailing was so loud, so hysterical, and so chilling that nearby patients were moved to other rooms and musicians were brought in to fill the halls with sounds other than cries. It didn't stop there. Far from it! The patient was from an expressive cultural tradition, and as the mourners intensely experienced their grief, the nurses were alarmed by this reaction. Family members flung themselves on top of her lifeless body, and at one point, the patient's mother wrapped herself in the patient's arms and bounced up and down in the bed, tossing both herself and the body from side to side.

Witnessing this made my palms sweaty. I thought I was going to throw up from the intensity of it. I stood frozen at the back of the room. The nurses wanted the poor chaplain—poor me—to intervene. But they don't teach you that in seminary. What was I supposed to do? *"Um, ma'am, just wondering if you might get up and let us call the funeral home or something. Any interest in grabbing lunch from the cafeteria downstairs? The food is really tasty today. I think it is a new chef."* What would that have looked like? It's not like she was hurting her daughter. Completely unsure of myself or the situation, I encouraged the staff to leave and stand outside the door. We did. Forty or so minutes later, after the musicians played a dozen songs, the family and the neighborhood emerged. They were composed.

The patient lay with a flower in her hands. They had brushed her hair and put a designer T-shirt on her so that she looked

7

like herself. Earlier that morning I had sat at my desk overlooking Long Island Sound, imagining a day filled with other people's grief. When confronted with something completely new, I had gotten out of the way and allowed it to be what it needed to be. I'm sure some other chaplain, nurse, or social worker would have dealt with this situation differently. However, for me, my decision was part of a paradigm shift in which I now firmly believe.

As a culture we tend to think that *grief is something controllable and if we contain it we can get back to our lives quickly.* Whereas, I think *grief is something that is organic and spontaneous and if we let it be what it needs to be, then healing can happen and flow through that authenticity and vulnerability.*

Grief is a normal part of the human experience. Allowing grief to be what it needs to be can enhance one's healing. Unfortunately, society is often uncomfortable with the ebb and flow that is grief.

We Americans, for the most part, like to think we are tidy. We spend billions each year on products to help us appear organized. Like many Americans, I buy plastic bins, shelving units, and closet organizers to keep up the illusion that my house will be neater, my life easier, and things a little more orderly. Grief is messy, and no matter how we look at its complexities, if we file it on a shelf in some stylish container, we will only stumble upon it at a later date when looking for something else.

In order to go any further in preparing ourselves to support a grieving child, we need to identify our grief triggers and prejudices and reflect on our own grief story. There in the depths of stories that have not been told in years, stories that may have become family secrets, aspects of a narrative that do not add up, and whatever fears surround our own mortality, we can better know ourselves and develop the empathy necessary to allow a child to fully experience his or her grief. Through that fully felt and supported grief experience, a grieving child can feel sadness and love at the same time, as he or she digests the complexities of death and finds hope in spite of it.

Kids Feel, Too

Knowledge is the most essential tool for any caregiver. Teachers, administrators, nurses, pediatricians, EMTs, police, psychologists, clergy, moms and dads, and anyone who interacts with children will be far more effective in their role if they become competent about children's grief. Unfortunately, many people are resistant or resist taking the time to become competent. Learning about children's grief is uncomfortable for some people because it acknowledges that many of us die young. It engages a difficult topic that our culture has decided to push aside, and it challenges many preconceived notions that we have accepted as the norm or, in some cases, as truth.

However, adults, especially those in positions or roles with power and impact on children, have a responsibility to gain and develop their knowledge. An inability or unwillingness to do so can have a lifelong effect on a child. It takes time to develop our grief knowledge, and it also takes a willingness to listen to, and be patient with, children. After my time at hospice, I joined a group of concerned parents in New Jersey who wanted to offer programs to grieving children. They hired me to create these programs at Good Grief, a nonprofit organization for children ages three to eighteen, young adults, and their surviving parent(s) or guardians. Good Grief advocates for adults to develop their grief knowledge. The organization has also grown rapidly in order to meet the needs of grieving children by providing a support system that is otherwise nonexistent in the lives of most grieving children.

In my role as an advocate for grieving children, I have learned that parents, teachers, and pastors seem to struggle most with shifting their expectations when around grief. Perhaps that shift is because they feel responsibility for the child. I think part of the inner turmoil many caregivers experience has to do with a need to feel in control of emotions and how they get expressed. I believe many people in authoritative roles like to see feelings expressed in a neat, orderly, and restrained way.

Often, when I am sitting with a bereaved parent and child, engrossed in an emotional or vulnerable conversation about the child's grief, the parent does all the talking on behalf of the child. The child, especially if he or she is a teen, just stares at the parent or me. Sometimes I can feel the contempt, shame, or disconnect that is happening in front of me as a result of a parent sharing intimate feelings or stories. The parent tells a story filled with his perspective on things while the child has a story of her own that she may not view in the same way as her parent. The child is voiceless while the parent talks about the child's outbursts, silence, or secrets.

When Evan and Emilia, his fifteen-year-old daughter, came to my office, Evan was a chatterbox. He was distraught over the death of his wife, who was killed in a taxi accident a few weeks beforehand. He went into elaborate detail about Emilia's withdrawal, her journal entries, her teacher's comments, her interactions with friends, what she ate, what she didn't eat, how often she showered, and so much more. Of course, he was coming at this from a place of fear and sincere worry about his daughter's well-being. He thought this one event, the painful death of her mother, was about to ruin her life. After he finished speaking, and as if he had said nothing at all, I turned to Emilia and asked, "Emilia, it's so good to meet you. I'm sorry that you are here. Please, tell me how you're feeling and what these last weeks have been like for you. I really want to hear how you are feeling." She perked up, completely aware that I was interested in her, her feelings, and her story as she saw it.

In the field of children's bereavement, it is often said that the children are the forgotten mourners. One reason the children are forgotten is because the adults like to do all the talking on their kids' behalf while the kids sit and listen to how someone else is seeing and telling their story. Perhaps that is because so much of a caregiver's response comes from a place of fear.

On an unusually warm winter afternoon, the mayor of a local town called to inform me that a student had killed herself after being bullied. The mayor asked me to reach out to the school, which I did promptly. At first, the school's administrators were interested in talking about the event and how to support the students. However, within a week's time the principal stopped returning my calls and e-mails. Eventually, she left a message on my voicemail, well after business hours, saying, "Thanks for your calls. I appreciate your reaching out. We're doing just fine here. Best wishes." Well, OK then. I guess they received a lot of support from somewhere else. Surely, they were not going to pretend this hadn't happened. Unfortunately, the latter is all too common, and many administrators, teachers, parents, and other authoritative people like to sweep death under the rug and act as if things are normal, as if this year is no different from the last.

Two months later I received a call from a guidance counselor requesting a workshop. First, she and the principal asked for an outline of the two-hour presentation. Silly me, I thought they wanted to talk about grief, supporting students, and healing after tragedy in the community. I was allowed to engage all my proposed topics *except* the ones that pertained to the student who took her life. That was an insane amount of fuel for my fire. I scrapped all of that content on my outline and resubmitted it. Then, thirty minutes into the presentation, I dove into the inferno!

My role as a grief educator is not to make friends, reinforce bad ideas, and encourage people's comfort at the expense of kids. So I set off some fireworks by providing knowledge and by asking questions about the student, the teachers' responses, and how the students were coping. Not surprisingly, the teachers and administrators were at complete odds. There were outbursts from those who had gained new insight from my presentation, which had completely contradicted the school's protocol up to this point—a protocol that had been one of silence and acting as if the student's death were irrelevant to the health of the student body. In fact, two days before my arrival, teachers had torn up a student's poem because it had referred to the girl who had taken her life. Now, they were hearing from me that their whole approach was backward and completely misinformed.

The administration was convinced, as so many misinformed administrations are, that if they talked about the girl's suicide and had a memorial service for her then a wave of copycats would follow and half the senior class would be dead because they wanted a memorial tree and attention, too. Instead of engaging the community's grief, the school administration had completely ignored it so as to avoid "glorifying the death." Now, if the student had been the star football player, killed in a car accident after a night of boozing on the town, would the school have responded in the same way? Probably not. The deceased would have gotten his memorial tree or whatever ritual the school was accustomed to doing. But suicide scares many people, and they do not understand it. There is a lot of fear about contagion, which is the belief that others will take their lives, too; but there is no scientific evidence that memorials or healthy expressions of mourning lead to contagion. It is nevertheless a belief that has shaped our reactions to suicide for years.

In front of the entire faculty, I asked the principal to define "glorification." I asked her whether she thought that ignoring the tragedy would prevent the kids from feeling, talking about it, and hurting because of it. I was met with silence.

Feelings are tricky things. Well, actually, they're not, if you are willing to engage them. Some people are terrified of being terrified or fear anger or loneliness, and some even fear happiness. There are a million and one ways in which we can either embrace or suppress feelings. But, if we do the latter, we are certain to find them again when we least expect it. They may stay quiet for years, but like a monster under the bed, they're going to pop out and scare us silly.

As individuals we can choose to suppress our feelings, but as adults we cannot allow our fears to force children to suppress theirs. It is an incredible power that we execute and force on children daily, without their permission. One might think that an event as great as the death of a parent or sibling might receive a more sophisticated response from adults, but we've grown accustomed to thinking adults know best and kids should conform to the status quo. However, grief is a good thing, and it serves a purpose. The role of the adult is not to fix it, take it away, or make it better. Rather, our role is to support the expression of feelings—all feelings—so that children can develop good coping skills that will help them for the rest of their lives.

This process of feeling is a complex one, and it looks different for every child, teen, and adult, despite the characteristics that our grief stories might share.

An eleven-year-old boy who is at Good Grief recently talked about feeling that his dad was disappointed in him. He told his peers, "When my dad was alive, I played basketball, tennis, football, baseball, and soccer. Now that he is dead I only like basketball. I think he is disappointed in me." Those are some big feelings for an eleven-year-old. His peers listened and were silent for a minute as they thought about his words and reflected on similar feelings.

That boy was met with a hug from his friend, who said, "I guess you'll never know; but tennis is stupid, anyhow." And there in that moment the boy realized, in some small way, that he could still live his life how he wanted and it didn't have to look like Dad prescribed. He smiled at his friend and said, "Yeah, you're totally right. I hate tennis, but basketball is awesome. Did you see the Celtics game?"

That boy's ability to express his feeling of disappointment without someone saying, "No, that's not true," or, "You shouldn't feel that way. That's silly. Your dad loved you," allowed him to arrive at a more authentic place. He was able to test the feeling with his peers, see if they could relate, and come to a conclusion on his own. His ability to come to a conclusion on his own was an important one. That does not mean an adult couldn't have facilitated that process; rather, it means he had the permission to do his grief work, think it through, feel the feelings, and explore what it meant to him.

Outside of the center I do not spend much time with the grieving children who go there, because I have very clear boundaries and because I don't see it as my role to socialize with families who come to Good Grief. Sometimes, however, I have rare opportunities for informal interactions. During the spring of 2012, as part of a fundraiser, I brought a family of four with me to Six Flags, an amusement park that lures many New Jersey, New York, Pennsylvania, and Connecticut children and adults.

I had a whole day planned for the three kids, the mom, and me. I had heard that the place was chock-full of fun rides, dramatically improved from when I was a kid. The prospect of spending the day at the park thrilled me. Much to my surprise, the kids were pretty terrified of roller coasters. They were more interested in what I thought of as the "baby rides." It started off as a day without a lot of promise.

I went to the park planning on having a blast and on completely taking advantage of an opportunity to spend the day playing with kids. I was eager, excited, and engrossed with reconnecting with my inner child. The trip to Six Flags was a much-needed break from the office and an easy way to have fun with the kids, who were a perfect excuse for my own childish behavior. However, because I was engrossed in my own adventures, I almost entirely missed what was going on with the kids.

The last time the children had been to the park was three years before with their dad. The kids weren't interested in exploring new rides. More than anything, they wanted to ride all the rides they remembered riding with Dad.

I'm not a huge fan of getting wet at amusement parks. I find it to be a nasty, chlorine-filled experience that I could do without. However, the kids remembered the log ride as being Dad's favorite. We rode that cursed ride five times. It is a long ride that ascends and then bumps around a large channel that winds its way to a drop. You end up getting soaked. Every time we got on the ride, around every turn, bump, and drop, the kids shared memories of Dad.

He had died a little more than a year before this day I spent at the park with his kids. His absence was painfully present. However, sloshing around in that wet log and riding the teacups and chugging cold beverages brought his presence back. His children could remember him. They could imagine him jumping into the log. They knew what he would have said. They told me what they would have told him. They talked about the painful day when he had dropped dead. Kids and adults alike overheard our conversation. Some looked uncomfortable; some were teary-eyed and empathetic. It felt like I was standing on the tracks with a roller coaster coming at me. I got out of the way and watched these kids do their grief work.

I easily could have put on the brakes by changing subjects—asking about school, talking about music, or introducing some other conversation. There are a thousand things I might have said and done to bring the whole thing to a screeching halt. I just got out of the way by listening, showing my interest, keeping up with them, getting wet, and letting them remember. And they said, "This is the most fun we've had in a long time. This day is amazing."

The day did not end there, though. The kids watched me get on roller coasters and laughed as the vertigo and nausea set in when I returned to them. They refused to participate in my roller-coaster extravaganza: "No way, man. I'll throw up. I'll boot everywhere. It's not happening!" That was their mantra, and they stuck to it. However, fifteen minutes before the park closed, they asked me if I was going to go on Kingda Ka. Kingda Ka is the tallest roller coaster in the world; and for its first five years of operation, it was the fastest in the world as well.

The ride uses a hydraulic launch mechanism to propel the cars 128 miles per hour up 456 feet of vertical track. Sometimes the cars do not make it to the top and fall backward, needing to be relaunched. It has vomit written all over its description. At first I told the kids that I wasn't doing it. I was sun fatigued, hungry, and ready to go home. But their interest was peaked in a way that caught my attention, so we walked over to the entrance. The boys marveled at it while their little sister shuddered with fear. "You guys look really interested in this ride. What are you going to tell your friends about it tomorrow?" Oops, I had planted the seed. "No way, Mr. Joe. We know what you're doing. That's terrifying. Maybe next time. We'll do it when we are bigger," they told me.

"OK guys, I'm not going to push you to do anything you don't want to do. I wonder, though, how you'd feel afterward having conquered this fear you've been thinking about all day. I wonder what that would feel like." As the words came out of my mouth, I also wondered what I was doing. I knew this meant I would be on that godforsaken death trap myself if they found the courage. The boys took each other by the hand, went into the bathroom, splashed water on their faces, and walked out like ghosts, actually flushed of color. "Let's go. We're doing this." I could not pause. I had to roll with it. Boy, did I feel sick to my stomach at that moment.

When it was our turn to get on the ride, the boys froze. The attendant shouted at us, "Get on the ride. It's your turn. You have to get on now!" I gave her an evil eye, feeling protective of the kids and terrified for myself. They waited until the next turn, and then we were locked in. Every word out of their eight- and twelve-year-old mouths was vulgar. I'm talking language you hear in Quentin Tarantino movies. When the ride started it felt like a plane taking off, except that we were completely exposed and launching straight into the air. Luckily, the thing was so fast that the ride was over in twenty-eight seconds. It was a combination of joy and hell all at once.

The boys exited the roller coaster and continued their vulgarities. The youngest said it had been the best moment of his life and vomited three times. He felt like he had conquered something incredible, something that gave him chills and made him sick to his stomach. I stood in shock. I do not know how I had gotten on that ride. The vertigo and nausea were brutal, and I was not sure how I would drive home. I felt like an old man. But the pride those boys felt in themselves was unbelievable. I had simply trusted the process and followed their lead. Every time I see them now, they recount that great flight to the top of Kingda Ka.

Grief can be a lot like a ride on Kingda Ka. For kids, grief is often very physical and can include bellyaches and vomiting. Grief is typified by intense feelings and emotions that are not easily articulated. The three-year-old who is grieving his mom might be able to tell you a little bit about it, but there is a good chance he will mostly feel it in his belly. When I was fourteen and wanted to talk about the death I had witnessed, and no one listened, it turned into an abdominal quagmire because that was the only place it could go. For kids who do not have the vocabulary to name feelings, the emotion turns into physical feeling. But the intensity of these feelings diminishes over time as a child develops coping skills and finds healthy ways to let the feelings out.

Unfortunately, without a good support system, grieving kids, particularly teens, are also susceptible to finding unhealthy ways of letting out and expressing their grief.

It is essential that we acknowledge that kids feel, too.

Kids will remember well into adulthood. Because of their feelings, they will remember who bullied them, who showed up, and who avoided them. I have met countless adults who can recount their childhood grief as if it were yesterday. How we support and care for grieving children and their emotional needs will follow them throughout their lives and affect their emotional selves, which is why we must be attuned to children's unique grief experience and be competent about grief.

Because of the impact of grief on a child's life, many mental health professionals have utilized this as an example of why we should treat grief and develop intervention strategies. However, we need to make a few crucial paradigm shifts before we can fully understand why grief does not require treatment.

Common belief: Grieving children need treatment as a result of the death they experienced in childhood.

Shift: Adults need to be educated about childhood bereavement so that they will stop interfering with children's grief experiences.

Common belief: Grief during childhood is bad or unnatural. It is a premature event that should be reserved for aging adults and thus is inherently traumatic.

Shift: Grief serves a healthy purpose that builds upon a child's resiliency, coping skills, and a more developed sense of self. Similarly, a child's grief work can prepare the child to better understand why there is suffering in the world and help him or her develop a capacity for empathy.

Common belief: Adults can teach children how to grieve and how to recover from trauma.

Shift: Children are great teachers when it comes to death, and they inherently have the tools they need in order to process and continue growing after experiencing a death.

To pathologize grief is to pathologize birth. That is to say, if we tell Matt that his grief needs treatment because he feels sad that Daddy cannot take him to the train museum anymore, then we might as well pathologize every other universal and natural human experience, including birth. Let's treat the newborns; after all, they did not ask to be born, the birthing process was traumatic, and that "major life event" has now set them up for immense suffering and the possibility of extreme dysfunction when they become adults. Birth and death are universal life experiences, not disorders.

The feelings that a child experiences during grief are normal. They are all normal feelings no matter the intensity or type of feeling, no matter their cause. For example, Tommy witnessed his dad die when debris flew through the car window and killed him. If Tommy is afraid to get in cars as a result of this incident, that is a normal feeling and reaction. I know I would be afraid; wouldn't you?

We can help Tommy find the courage, in his own time, to sit in the car. We can help him sit in the car when it drives down the driveway. We can support him by setting up goals, such as going for a ride around the block, and finding ways to build upon safe experiences. We do not need to treat or fix Tommy because he is frightened as a result of a scary experience. He needs love, support, understanding, and a little encouragement.

When Eve, a five-year-old who attends Good Grief, cries every time Dad makes her go to the doctor, a place she thinks one goes to die when sick, that is a normal and rational response. Eve remembers all the doctor visits with Mom. She remembers the hospital and the shots, the tears, and all the sadness that filled her house and the hospital rooms. As Eve tries to understand why Mommy is buried in the cemetery, she is processing all the events and people that were involved in Mom's death. There were a lot of doctors. Now she is scared of doctors—a normal reaction.

Eve was also at one time scared of the kitchenette in the room where she and her Good Grief friends play. The night Mommy died, Daddy threw pots and pans and sobbed in the kitchen. Her trepidation did not mean that we needed to keep Eve away from the kitchenette or never teach her how to cook. Rather, moving at her own pace, Eve was able to see the other kids playing and having fun with plastic strudel. She worked her way over and fiddled with some pots. Soon she was telling the story of Daddy's sadness. And from there, she baked a dozen plastic muffins, which had been Mommy's favorite—a normal reaction.

Currently, adults are at odds with two philosophical approaches to parenting: (1) a lot of structure and regimentation, and (2) allowing kids to be whatever and however they want to be with a fullness of expression, including expression through dress, music, dance, makeup, tattoos, piercings, and sexual experimentation. There are some interesting parallels between the two approaches, and I believe a blend of both makes for a healthy environment.

Kids like boundaries and a little structure. Having limits helps a child feel safe, nurtured, and looked after. When an adult steps in and says, "You've already eaten one bag of candy today; no more," that's a good thing. A child knows that if she eats five bags of candy, it means no one is paying attention, and that implies the so-called loving adults in her life might not actually care about her and might not be there when she is getting herself in real trouble. There is room to set limits without nagging, controlling, or getting in the way of a child's development.

Similarly, kids need to know that they can share their truest fears, express their quirks, and talk about those things that are most important to them, without judgment. Providing the space and time for children to be themselves—whether that means being silly, rambunctious, serious, or otherwise—affirms a child's sense of self. Children know who they are and have a good sense of what they think, even if the latter is a blip on the screen during a developmental stage or rebellion. If we allow that expression to come out and have its place—by giving children permission to be themselves—kids are less likely to feel ashamed and to express feelings, fears, and personality traits in an unhealthy or counterproductive way.

When Gulian first came to Good Grief, she was the embodiment of that TV character Punky Brewster. Everything about Gulian screamed 1984—leotards, neon, mismatched socks, and grunge. She was eight. Her dad had died because of a parachute malfunction while skydiving. Gulian had always been a spunky kid, even after her dad died. As she got older she became more self-conscious, and kids teased her about her outfits. The day she started wearing blue jeans, matching sneakers, and clean T-shirts, she tucked away her spunk. When the other kids were sitting around, she stayed back and waited until she felt safe joining in. When the group was acting completely free-spirited and unaware of their silliness, Gulian was quick to jump into this carefree and nonjudgmental environment and her spunk returned.

Gulian's suppressed spunk was much like David's apprehension to talk about his mom. David experiences shame when talking about his mom, because people have told him that he uses her as an excuse to skip homework and coast through life. He has also been told that he should be "over" his mom's death by now. It has been three years, and his friends don't think he should talk about her anymore. David, of course, strongly disagrees, but instead of fighting back for his right to express himself, he experiences shame when he feels his grief and wants to talk about it.

Children and teens have rich inner and emotional lives. The depths and intensity of those inner lives are even greater after experiencing the death of a loved one or other important person. Rather than adults telling a child how to feel, or attempting to change the quality or nature of those feelings, caregivers can enliven and empower the complexity of a child's feelings by providing the space and time for them to come to full fruition and full expression.

Although we seem to think that death is for the old and that adults are best equipped for tragedies, children are wildly resilient and know a great deal about life and death. Whether we are hardwired with this information or quickly absorb data about relationships and loss, the outcome does not change. Whether we are born knowing that we will die or we learn about grief from having greedy playmates steal our rattles and toys, we land in the same place. We can understand a challenge and simultaneously have faith in our ability to resolve it. Whereas we adults tend to be shaken by grief and struggle to wrap our minds around the death of a loved one, a child absorbs fragments of the information while working to ensure that his or her basic needs will be met and that he or she will not be abandoned. Often, children inquire about the death and express their grief one morsel at a time.

Adults do not work through their grief at the same pace and in the same way that kids do. Children often move through grief slowly, in increments, and from side angles. As a result, many adults are baffled or enraged by what they see when they tell a child, "Your mommy died." When Sally told Jessica that Dad had had a heart attack during Mass that Sunday morning, Jessica looked blankly at Sally and cried what Sally described as "crocodile tears." When Sally told me this story, she said, "How could she just look at me? She and her father were inseparable. It's like he didn't even matter. She wanted to go to softball practice that afternoon!"

Jessica, nine-years-old at the time, was surrounded by adults who thought either that she did not feel anything or that the feelings were simply selfish. This went on for several weeks before Sally reached out for help. Unfortunately, many grieving kids find themselves in households where the adults have expectations that children are not in fact capable—not physiologically capable—of meeting. How a child is able to respond to grief depends on where he or she is developmentally.

Although we may have our own ideas about what a child's grief should look like, a child's grief work is an important process that will unfold no matter the roadblocks we put up or the attempts we make to relieve the pain. The question at hand is whether the adults will facilitate healthy or unhealthy coping.

As a result of experiencing a death during childhood, kids are confronted with some challenging questions at a young age. These are not bad questions, even though they may be difficult questions or questions without an answer. They are simply questions that engage the universal human experience and explore how life works (or doesn't).

Jeff is a facilitator at Good Grief. Both of his parents died when he was a child. Now, as an adult, he is twenty years older than his dad had been when he died. Jeff and I went out for lunch a few years ago, and he told me, "I would do anything to have had my dad into adulthood. There is nothing I wouldn't do to have both my parents back. But, you know what? I wouldn't be who I am today if my life had turned out 'perfect,' or however it was expected to turn out." And that is a golden moment. Not everyone arrives there or needs to come to the same conclusion as Jeff. But it is common for individuals to get a little distance, reassess their life's path, and see that their tragedy is an integral part of how they experience the world.

I have heard too many adults say things like, "Don't worry. There is a reason this happened. God wouldn't give you more than you could handle, and you'll be stronger because of it!" These clichéd attempts at telling children how to make meaning out of their stories are pervasive. Though well intentioned, unfortunately such patronizing statements disaffirm a child's grief experience and grief work precisely because these assertions seem to be easy and universal. Each child's unique grief work is important, even if it sounds foolish or silly, irrational or illogical, to adult ears. Some children experience these platitudes as confusing because the children's grief seems far more difficult and intense than these answers suggest. Grief eludes consoling explanations, and this absurdity turns out to be part of grief's beauty. By grieving we mull over the complexities of our life story and how we and the dead fit into a world that now looks and feels different, given the presence of absence. When we persist with simplistic answers, we deny our children the opportunity that grief presents to develop their own complex and authentic worldview.

I'm often asked if a six-month-old child can grieve. Sometimes people are shocked that Good Grief provides support even for three-year-olds. "Oh, what could they possibly understand? They just play," I am told more frequently than I care to hear. An infant grieves the death of her mother. She grieves because of her mother's absence. Mommy's familiar smell, skin, touch, voice, and affection are gone. Infants grieve. It might look like colic, withdrawal, or difficulty sleeping, but nonetheless, it is grief.

Kids of all ages feel and experience grief. In the presence of absence, children can be with and move through that grief if those who are entrusted with their care show up, listen, affirm their many feelings, and allow them to be wherever they need to be in their grief work.

Chapter 3

Myths

In 1969 Swiss, psychiatrist Elisabeth Kübler-Ross made a bit of a mess. She is, it seems, the forever misquoted and misunderstood creator of the "Five Stages of Grief." Her five stages are sound bites on local news networks and buzzwords in sitcoms, traipsed around classrooms and doctors' offices alike as people attempt to articulate the grieving process. The Kübler-Ross model appeared in her groundbreaking book *On Death and Dying,* which was a book that actually did a lot of good for Americans who had grown accustomed to ignoring death's pervasive presence. Kübler-Ross, by all means, made a gigantic impact on the American treatment of death. Her work helped Florence Wald, Dean of Yale School of Nursing, bring hospice to the United States. The hospice that Wald founded in Connecticut happens to be the same place where I companioned and supported patients for four years.

The problem with Kübler-Ross's model is that it has been understood, most often by lay people, as a linear trajectory for the grieving process. If you stop someone on the street and ask him about the five stages, there is a good chance he will know what they are but will not be able to tell you how he learned about them or what their relevance is. If you do not know these five stages, then consider yourself a clean slate with the ability to catch up to new and better ideas. And although there has been a lot of subsequent research concerning the experience of grief, Kübler-Ross's persists in our cultural imagination.

Kübler-Ross's five stages pertaining to dying are: denial, anger, bargaining, depression, and acceptance. However, many people apply these stages to bereavement, as if to suggest that a bereaved person must first deny the death and then work his or her way through a prescribed experience until arriving at acceptance or "moving on." Kübler-Ross, however, offered her stages as a way to understand what a dying person goes through in the face of his or her own imminent extinction.

Yet, even as the stages pertain to dying, they are only partially accurate. Not everyone accepts that he or she is dying; not everyone bargains; not everyone feels anger. The stages, in my opinion, are merely possible characteristics of the dying experience—some shoes fit; many don't. However, popular culture has accepted the five stages as the norm, as basic and necessary protocol. These assumptions and misunderstandings have led to a big mess, which affects kids negatively. When children express their grief in ways that make adults feel uncomfortable, many adults reach for Kübler-Ross's insights and apply them thoughtlessly. Often, believing acceptance to be the end goal of grief, a caring guidance counselor or teacher tries tirelessly to make the child accept the death and move on.

As a result of Kübler-Ross's model, Americans have created many misleading paradigms about the grief experience. We see grief as a linear experience with checkpoints, perhaps milestones that map progress, until we finally arrive at a time when our grief file can be stamped with "cured" and life resumes as normal. We expect grief to have a direction; a rhythm; and most important, a conclusion. It seems that we want order to be restored after the chaos that can accompany a person's grief. However, this approach doesn't leave room for the organic and unpredictable components of grief. This false sense of order is unrealistic; uncommon; and, I might go as far as to say, unnatural.

When we create these false expectations, we hurt the bereaved, who feel like failures. I so often hear: "Something is wrong with me." The bereaved experience a sense of failure or "wrongness" because they have been led to believe that their grief is a trajectory that moves through milestones, meets goals, and concludes with a thunderous, cathartic applause as a finish line is crossed and the person who died is a distant memory whose death can no longer cause pain.

Whereas the stages might suggest a linear order, I see grief as a spiral that goes up, down, and all around. It overlaps; goes backward; wanders far from the path and then jumps back on again, only to revisit the beginning even though it appeared that the grief was finished. That type of unpredictability and individuality makes people anxious. It makes those who want to help or "fix" the bereaved uncomfortable, and it often makes the bereaved feel unsure of themselves because they thought they were further along.

For a grieving child, grief emerges and reemerges in new ways as the child matures and goes through different developmental stages, which I will set forth shortly.

A five-year-old boy was playing in the toy kitchen at the center and pushed a grocery cart up to my leg. He bumped it into my shin to hear me shriek, which I did, not because it hurt but to amuse him. "Grocery store is the worst for Daddy. He buys me and Mom's favorite cereal, Frosted Flakes. He cries every time. Now I eat Fruit Loops because Daddy is sad." And then he returned to the kitchen to fix a plate of plastic chicken and corn. Similarly, a kid could be having the best time playing soccer. She looks to the left and sees a dad hugging her teammate. Then come the waterworks—tears, pouting, hysteria—or detached silence. These grief triggers are always available, present at any moment, even the most unexpected. That is what makes grief so organic, nonlinear, and hardly controllable.

I believe part of the reason we like the idea of linear grief, even though so many people have experienced and witnessed its circular patterns, is because we like to be in control of emotions, especially our children's reactions and outbursts or grief bursts. It gives us a sense of safety, even if it's false.

Continuing Bonds

Grief is not a thing of the past, which in part is why it doesn't function linearly. It is of the past, present, and future. Its ongoing presence is of great importance to children. Children feel safe when they feel a sense of connection to the past and a connection to the person who died. The continuum of a child's life story, the time when Mom was alive to the time when she is not, allows for consistency and an ongoing relationship with the deceased, rather than tucking the dead away in the past.

This need for chronological connection also emerges in graduation season. What does a high school look like in May or June? We see yearbooks, good-bye parties, graduation parties, celebration, speeches about the future, hope for unknown possibilities ahead, and so on. Half the time, high school seniors even engage in these rituals with people they never liked, as if the past four years of competition and rivalry meant nothing. This life transition is loaded with ritual, remembrance, and a sense of connection. Before moving forward into the next phase of life, many high school kids do all they can to establish a sense of connection to the last eighteen years of their life. This connection becomes a comfort in the face of the scary unknown that will be unfolding in August or September, perhaps thousands of miles away from home and everything familiar.

Experiencing a connection to the past is important for many children as they move forward, in this case with rebuilding their lives, family unit, and sense of self. Without control over the transitions themselves, transitional rituals help us process events, express feelings, remember, honor, celebrate, let go, and hold on.

Funerals

I'm often met with the question of whether a child should attend a funeral. I've heard all sorts of opinions about why they should not and I have yet to hear one that merits further thought. Here is why: kids are no less capable of participating, no less resilient, and no more susceptible to grief than anyone else.

In 2008 I was training a group of bereavement facilitators. During an activity that captured the trainees' stories and grief, one participant shared a story from 1953. Kerry was six years old when her mother died of breast cancer. Kerry had seen her mom in the hospital a few times before her mother died. On the morning her mom died, Kerry had been staying over at her cousin's house. A family meeting was called, and the house became filled with grandparents, aunts, uncles, cousins, and a few close family friends. They told Kerry and her younger brother that Mommy had died. Kerry does not remember her reaction to the news, but she does remember the adults informing her that she would remain with her cousins for the week and then return home after the funeral, which she was not invited to attend or participate in.

Fifty-five years later, Kerry sobbed as she recounted the event and her feelings about the funeral that she was not allowed to attend. She has carried feelings of resentment with her for half a century because she was excluded. As she describes it, the entire town showed up for the funeral. People who did not even know her mom went to the funeral to show their support. Folk from all over walked past her casket, kneeled before her body, escorted her into a church, and then buried her. But Kerry, her own flesh and blood, was left with cousins to eat peanut butter and jelly and watch *The Andy Griffith Show* while the most important person in her childhood was remembered and returned to the earth. "I will never forget that. I will never let this go," she told the group.

Certainly Kerry's dad had good intentions in leaving his daughter out of her mother's funeral, just as a similarly well-intentioned grandmother recently called me for advice. Her daughter and son-in-law had gotten into a fight that turned physical and concluded with Dad shooting Mom in the face. When I received this call, Dad was in the county jail, Mom was at the funeral home, and the kids were in the care of their grandparents. The funeral was the next day. Grandma was not planning on allowing the kids to attend the funeral. Her friends and many family members supported the decision. However, the kids would have none of it. They wanted in, and these six- and nine-year-old children were prepared to storm the funeral home with their blankies in hand. Something inside the grandmother told her to pick up the phone.

"What are the kids telling you?" I asked. "And what have you told them?" The children had witnessed the fighting and had seen the aftermath of Mom in the kitchen.

"The kids want to see their mother and go to the funeral. They just cry and yell at me when I try to explain why they can't. They've gone through enough. Just tell me what to do. It would be terrible to bring them, right?"

So many people in a time of grief, which is a heightened and incredibly vulnerable time, want someone else to lead them—or drag them—through, because they cannot see a way beyond the pain.

I explained to Grandma that she had not done anything wrong. I commended her for reaching out for help and for trying so hard while she was grieving the loss of her daughter. I then told her about Kerry and countless other adults who resented and distrusted the adults who forbade their participation in a funeral.

Why would we prohibit a child from attending a funeral? Why does the entire town get to show up while the kids are forced to stay at home or are sent away for a week?

"Tell the children," I said to that grandmother, "in spurts, following their lead. Be in tune with what they want and need to know, and explain what they'll see. Don't go into tons of detail unless they ask for it."

In this case, the family was Roman Catholic. First up was a four-hour wake. "Practice with me," I told her. We went through the ritual moment by moment. She then got off the phone and made a decision that directly affected the children's grief and probably her ability to raise them as a trusted and caring figure in their lives.

"Kids, do you still want to go to the funeral?" she asked. And exuberantly they replied, "Yes!"

She then walked through the script she and I had crafted on the phone:

1. "Tomorrow we are going to go to what is called a wake. Grandma and Grandpa asked the man who works at the funeral home to put Mommy in a wooden casket. The casket will look like a box, and Mommy will be wearing the dress you and Daddy bought her for Mother's Day last year. You'll be able to see her arms and head. The lid of the casket will cover her feet, like a half-open jewelry box. There will be a lot of people there. If you get tired or want to play, you can

35

leave or go into another room, because this place where we are going is big like a house."

2. Wait. What do the kids say in response? Do they have questions? Do they need to process the information and go play before additional information is provided?

3. "OK, then the next day we are going to go to church and will bring Mommy with us. The priest will say prayers for her, and Grandma and Grandpa will probably look sad because we miss your Mommy."

4. Wait. What do the kids say in response? Do they have questions? Do they need to process the information and go play before additional information is provided?

5. "After church, we are going to go to the cemetery and will bring Mommy with us. Do you know what a cemetery is?

6. "The men who work at the cemetery will put Mommy's casket in the earth, just like you guys did with Daddy when Lucky died two summers ago. We will visit Mommy there and bring flowers, just like you did for Lucky."

7. Wait. "If you change your mind, I've asked Ms. Jessica to bring you home or take you out for ice cream. You just tell Ms. Jessica anything you need and she'll help you."

The kids did not have a lot of questions when they were told about the funeral. When they arrived at the funeral home the next day, they wanted to know why Mommy was cold and her face looked different. Grandma explained that we get cold and look different when we die. That's all the kids wanted to know at the time.

I've been pressed on this many times, especially by people arguing that cultural traditions need to be taken into consideration. Some people have fiercely argued that some cultures are too expressive during their rituals and that extreme vocalizations or physical expressions can cause a child trauma. I'll discuss trauma shortly to demonstrate why concerns about trauma are misplaced. Cultural consideration is important, but I see it much differently from those who want to prevent a child's participation because of cultural traditions.

Traditions and cultures are just that, because they have been passed down from one generation to the next. Within a particular group, they are norms, often practiced during a religious, cultural, or aging transition or milestone, including birth and death. I think there is room for modification or new traditions if the current practice is not inclusive of children. If someone feels strongly that his or her ritual is not the right fit for a child, I encourage consideration of these questions:

1. How do you expect the next generation to learn your ritual?

2. If you are that concerned about your tradition or ritual negatively affecting a child, then why are you doing it?

3. How will a child feel about the ritual, after being prohibited from participating in it as a child, when your culture deems it appropriate to participate in the ritual?

4. Is there a way to adjust your rituals to accommodate children?

5. Should you consider a new or modified ritual to better include children? Or should you consider a separate ritual for kids?

Similarly, adults can explain rituals to children, and if a particular ritual is as big and scary as the adults perceive it to be, a child can opt out. Children can understand wailing and shouting, and we adults can prepare them to witness such expressions by describing them and sharing why such traditions exist.

When I was eight or nine, my grandmother's brother died of a heart attack. He was a great guy, and I spent a fair amount of time with Uncle Joe, especially when I visited my grandparents for the weekend. When he died, someone told my parents that they should not bring my sister and me, as we went everywhere with my parents and would certainly show up at the wake and the funeral. So, we were left at home. My parents explained that Italians wail and that people were worried that it would be upsetting to us. The funeral, as a result, was a kid-free farewell. I imagined chairs getting thrown, a casket processing through the streets on top of shoulders, and my grandmother fainting into the arms of my grandfather. I do not believe that is what happened, but in 2009, when my grandfather died, I witnessed what Uncle Joe's funeral probably had looked like years before.

My grandmother wailed. She shouted and cried when we closed my grandfather's casket, when the Mass ended, and when we lowered him into his grave. It was wonderfully real. My frail grandmother was expressing everything we felt. Her grief became public in the form of mourning, and I could relate to those deep, belly wails. Many of us joined in because her mourning gave us permission to do so. I could have handled the wailing if I had seen it when I was eight. In fact, it would have taught me about grief. I wish I had witnessed my family's mourning years prior.

Funerals can help children do their grief work if the children themselves have a voice and a choice. Some kids will not want to participate in a funeral, and that is OK as long as they have the information they need to make that decision. The majority of children, however, will want to be there each and every step of the way. And they will want to talk about it, explore the meaning of it, question the process, and revisit the ritual in the future.

Some years back, a mom and her daughter came running into Good Grief. Alexis had just asked a big question: "Where is Daddy?" She meant literally, where is he physically located? The last time Alexis saw Daddy was at the church after the wake and the funeral service. Most of her Good Grief friends talked about going to the cemetery to visit their dads, but Alexis had never gone to the cemetery, and she wanted to know why.

Mom was caught off guard and said, "Honey, we cremated daddy and he is in my closet."

Alexis was befuddled. "What's cremation?"

Mom did not know how to respond. "Well, we'll be at Good Grief in a few minutes. Why don't you ask them?" And there they were, staring at us with a mouthful of questions and fear.

At first the staff did not respond. No one knew what narrative had led up to that moment. What had she been told in the car? What had she been told after the funeral? What had Alexis been led to believe over the past year?

"You know, Alexis, a couple of kids in group know what cremation is. Why don't you ask them, and if you still have questions I promise I'll answer them the best I can. They may be more helpful than me," one of our staff said. Alexis was fine with that response. She got everything she needed from her peers as they shared stories about the funerals and what had happened with the bodies of those they loved. Some children talked about visiting the cemetery, whereas others talked about scattering the remains of the person who had died and described how the ashes had looked and felt.

However, I was a little worried about Mom and how she was feeling. I was not sure that she had fully reflected on her decision to store Dad in the closet and not tell the kids. Now that they had that information, she had some other things to think about. So, I reached out to her to follow up.

Let's say that Mom left Dad in the closet, making him this mystery in a box. Well, curious kids can get themselves in trouble while trying to put together pieces of a puzzle. Imagine this, if my call were a little too late:

Mom goes out for girls' night. She is hanging out with friends and getting a much-needed break from her grief and parenting.

The babysitter thinks the kids are playing dress-up in Mommy's closet. Oh, but the temptation that is before them when they see that box on the top shelf, right there next to Dad's photo, is too great. Alexis yells at her brother to balance her as she reaches for the box. "Got it!" she exclaims. She turns it on its side and then on its belly to examine the thing. *Well, how does Dad fit into this?* she thinks. She notices the large screw on the bottom, and like any savvy eight-year-old, she takes Mom's brooch and uses it to unscrew the bottom of the urn. There, inside the box, is a bag of ashes. They're stuffed in there pretty tightly, which she does not realize. She gives it a tug, but that plastic bag is not built like the sturdy freezer bags that Mom stores her pasta sauce in. Yes, that pretty pink dress and the lipstick all over her face are now caked in white ash. Alexis panics.

The freak-out that ensues has nothing to do with Dad's ashes being spilled everywhere. She is just worried about getting in trouble. So quickly she puts the box back together and gets it back on the shelf. Later, the babysitter finds Alexis and her brother with a dustpan over the toilet, disposing of the mess Dad made.

Imagine Mom's girls' night out. Imagine Alexis's feelings when she later understands what just happened.

It would take a lot of courage for a parent to think quickly and find a way to work with an accident so that the kids would not feel incredible guilt and shame for exploring what it meant when Mommy said, "Daddy was cremated and he is in the closet." Adults can try to keep secrets about death or avoid the facts and details that children seek, but kids want to know and understand. Grieving kids will be healthier if we, the adults, are honest and earnest in helping them understand life and death—even if we are not sure what to make of them, either.

When I met Brenda and her three-year-old daughter, Lisa, I was not sure what to expect. Brenda was looking for support after her infant, Brady, had died from birth complications. Brenda and her husband, Bentley, had visited Brady in the hospital for three months as he fought pneumonia and every virus that could squirm its way into his struggling body. Lisa was with her mom most days when they frequented the hospital. However, she was not there the day Brady died.

Lisa had been off charming some friends; I imagine she was dressed like a princess, twirling in her ruby slippers. Lisa is a playful, giddy kid who loves girly glamour. While Lisa was at her friends', Bentley and Brenda were preparing to say good-bye to their three-month-old boy, who had taken a rapid turn for the worse.

Devastated, Brenda knew that she needed help while Bentley steered clear of his grief. So, Brenda found Good Grief.

Sitting in my office, Brenda recounted what had happened only a few weeks before. As we spoke, Lisa rearranged the antique dollhouse and got everything in order. As Mom cried, Lisa looked up and said, "It's OK, Mommy. I miss baby Brady, too!" Inevitably, Mom cried more, knowing that her daughter was also hurting. She then went on to tell me a story that reflected her sound instincts.

After Brady died, the family returned home and sat Lisa down in the family room to tell her the news. As they shared the words "Baby Brady died," Lisa looked around at all the adults who were crying and watching her reaction. She picked up a couple of dolls, stared at them for a few moments, and then looked back at her mom: "But, Mom, I didn't get to tell baby Brady good-bye."

On the day that Brady was to be cremated, Lisa and Brenda were driving around town doing errands for the memorial service when Lisa reminded Brenda that she had not gotten to say good-bye. Completely unsure of herself and the situation, Brenda immediately called the funeral home and said, "My daughter needs to say good-bye. We're coming over."

When Brenda and Lisa arrived at the funeral home, staff members took them to a room where they had wrapped Brady in a blanket. Without hesitation, Lisa rushed over to him and picked him up. She held him tight, kissing his forehead over and over. "I'm going to miss you, baby Brady. I'm going to miss you soooooo much." And then she returned him to the table and asked, "Mom, can we go get ice cream now?" And in that moment, which three years later she still recounts as one of her clearest memories with Brady, Lisa was able to get a grief need met.

Unfortunately, many mothers would not follow their instincts, as Brenda did, because they'd be afraid that the experience would be "traumatic." The language of trauma is common terminology even though most people don't understand it and make assumptions about its effects or long-term impact on a child.

Words People Love and Their Corresponding Labels

The lay people and professionals who want to define all grief as trauma or say that attending a funeral is traumatic for a child do not understand trauma or the differences between traumatology, which is the study of trauma, and thanantology, which is the study of death. The first issue at hand is defining trauma. What differentiates the traumatic event from nontraumatic? How, specifically, does that apply to death and grief?

First, there has been a shift in traumatology from defining particular events as traumatic to defining trauma through the individual's perception. In other words, trauma has gone from a universal experience to an individual perception. Consequently, not everyone involved in a car wreck is traumatized, but some people in car wrecks experience trauma because of how they perceive and interpret that event. But, again, what is trauma?

The word *trauma* is derived from the Greek word meaning "wound." When I think of the word *wound* I think of ripping, tearing, breaking, and piercing. *Trauma* refers to an emotional wound. Each of us experiences our emotions differently, thus making trauma an individual perception. How can we differentiate the woundedness of trauma from the intensity that is grief, in order to understand the difference between these intense physical and emotional reactions to a death?

To help us better understand traumatology, the *DSM-IV* (*Diagnostic and Statistical Manual of Mental Disorders*), which is what the American Psychiatric Association uses to diagnose disorders, says this about post-traumatic stress disorder (these symptoms occur for more than a month and affect daily life):

Criterion A: Stressor

The person has been exposed to a traumatic event in which both of the following have been present:

1. The person has experienced, witnessed, or been confronted with an event or events that involve actual or threatened death or serious injury, or a threat to the physical integrity of oneself or others.

2. The person's response involved intense fear, helplessness, or horror.

Criterion B: Intrusive Recollection

The traumatic event is persistently re-experienced in at least **one** of the following ways:

1. Recurrent and intrusive distressing recollections of the event, including images, thoughts, or perceptions.

2. Recurrent distressing dreams of the event.

3. Acting or feeling as if the traumatic event were recurring. . . . Intense psychological distress at exposure to internal or external cues that symbolize or resemble an aspect of the traumatic event.

4. Physiological reactivity upon exposure to internal or external cues that symbolize or resemble an aspect of the traumatic event.

Criterion C: Avoidant/Numbing

Persistent avoidance of stimuli associated with the trauma and numbing of general responsiveness (not present before the trauma), as indicated by at least **three** of the following:

1. Efforts to avoid thoughts, feelings, or conversations associated with the trauma

2. Efforts to avoid activities, places, or people that arouse recollections of the trauma

3. Inability to recall an important aspect of the trauma

4. Markedly diminished interest or participation in significant activities

5. Feeling of detachment or estrangement from others

6. Restricted range of affect

7. Sense of foreshortened future

Criterion D: Hyper-arousal

Persistent symptoms of increasing arousal (not present before the trauma), indicated by at least **two** of the following:

1. Difficulty falling or staying asleep

2. Irritability or outbursts of anger

3. Difficulty concentrating

4. Hyper-vigilance

5. Exaggerated startle response [1]

The fact that there is not much collaboration between thanatologists and traumatologists is a huge problem. The problem is that a lot of grief looks like trauma, and there is overlap between trauma and grief. Most trauma includes grief.

Let's look at Criterion D for an example. A lot of kids wet the bed, have difficulty sleeping, have outbursts because they don't have the words to articulate their feelings, and have difficulty concentrating in school because they are preoccupied with their feelings and the disarray that might permeate their lives. I believe the *DSM* definition of PTSD is written so broadly that it catches other kinds of behaviors, which we know from experience are normal and associated with grief. The downside of this is that we then pathologize and psychologize normal grief behaviors in ways that might tempt adults to treat grieving kids as if they were special or different and in need of intervention (or even medication), which in turn can alienate a child and double his sense of isolation after a loss.

Let's look at Criterion C next. After Jack's mom died, he wanted to be alone in his room to look at her pictures and listen to her favorite music. He didn't have a lot of interest in spending time with his peers. He felt that they did not understand him and were immature. They complained about "stupid stuff," and he now felt like he understood "real suffering" and "real problems." When Jack did hang out with friends, he found them to be insensitive. They often spent time together without him and made him feel different. His normal behavioral patterns, which he had exhibited before Mom's death, were gone. Jack is not going to be just like he was before Mom died. He will be similar to that person, but he has changed as a result of this event and its impact on his daily life. Is that a pathology? I do not think so. That is a normal characteristic of the grief experience. Could it be trauma?

Now, what about seventeen-year-old Daniel, who came home from school in the middle of September and found his mother dead? He knew his mom was sad and that his parents had been fighting. He did not expect to come home and stick his key into the lock only to find the door jammed. Through the crack of the slightly opened door, which had been blocked with a kitchen chair, he saw his mother hanging. With brute force he kicked down the door and rushed to his dead mother, who was hanging from his chin bar, the same chin bar that had given him the strength to break down the door. Daniel called his dad (who would later arrive at a scene filled with cops and firefighters), and said, "I love you, and what I'm going to say is going to hurt so bad."

When his dad arrived, Daniel ran to him and cried in his arms. His dad said, "Son, I love you, but it's not all going to be OK." Everything else that followed that day was normal. Daniel's response to hearing the news, and all the feelings and actions that happened next, were normal. They were normal for Daniel, his story, and his unique grief work because each characteristic of his grief was part of his grieving process. Was that event traumatic? Perhaps it was traumatic for Daniel, but that does not mean his reactions to his mom's death were a pathology or abnormal.

The traumatic response is normal; perhaps, we have become dependent on the word as a way to talk about the intense feelings we experience after intense events. So, if trauma and grief are normal, you may be wondering why it is so important that we do not label and assume that all grief is traumatic. I think it is important because people make assumptions about how an individual perceives and experiences that so-called traumatic event. They interact with the grieving child, and make decisions on behalf of the child, based on those assumptions. Similarly, misinformation about trauma could lead to assumptions that in turn could easily lead to treatment, which could include therapy, drugs, or a host of labels that are rooted in stigmas and erroneous ideas about mental illness. This is most likely to happen if the bereaved encounters a professional—a therapist or pediatrician—who is uninformed about the characteristics and intensity of grief.

We must remain cautious of labels and assumptions in order to prevent a universal life experience from becoming a disorder or being medically treated because of ignorance regarding grief. If the latter occurs, every well-meaning somebody will try to fix grief by getting in its way and throwing drugs and money at it, only to find that grief will still remain. But at what cost to the children as each child is pathologized and each feels all the more different from his or her peers than before?

I do not doubt that trauma is real or that some people experience a traumatic response as part of their grief. However, the two are not synonymous. The event does not have to be catastrophic to be traumatic. Watching a parent slowly die of cancer can be traumatic for a child, if that is how the child perceives it.

Normalizing Death and Grief

Remember Tommy, the boy who saw debris fly through the car window and kill his dad? He was afraid to get in a car. That was normal. He comes to Good Grief and never misses a group. This requires him to get in a car. Is he traumatized based only on whether he can or cannot get into a car and come to Good Grief? Based on the intensity and horror of that event, many people easily assume and label that experience as traumatic.

Dad dying was a type of wound or injury to Tommy's emotional self. It affects him daily, though it won't necessarily affect him forever. Tommy loved his dad very much. He will tell anybody who expresses interest in his dad how much his dad was loved. The question remains: Was Tommy traumatized? I believe only Tommy can say. If he cannot articulate it, then he might show us in other ways, such as through play with his peers.

I do not believe we can extract trauma from grief, but not everyone who grieves is traumatized. For me, in my attempts to understand a child's reaction to an intense experience like death, I propose this simple approach to move past labels: Are the coping strategies healthy or unhealthy? Is the teenager seeking help, getting support from friends, and making small efforts to find a daily routine after the death? Or is the teenager smoking marijuana and sneaking into the woods to drink as a way to cope with the pain? All of these responses are normal, but some of them require intervention and additional support to prevent unhealthy patterns of coping. I do not believe the unhealthy choices are pathological choices, though they might lead to unhealthy coping. Again, the issue for me lies in the expression of unhealthy behaviors and not in our assumptions about the psycho-emotional effects of a particular experience.

I believe lay people and some professionals analyze intense events as trauma because, culturally speaking, we think a child will be messed up after a parent dies: "Oh my God, there goes another kid lost to a dysfunctional life now that her parent has died." As a result of this preconception and our own anxiety about the long-term effects of childhood grief, we can easily use language we do not fully understand, labeling people and events as traumatized and traumatic. Before relying on this easy vocabulary, we should be mindful of labeling an experience as fundamental and complex as grief. Labels and their accompanying assumptions or prejudices stick, and kids begin to view their lives through the labels adults have attached to them.

Grief and Emotional Growth

Death usually has a tremendous impact on the daily lives of children, but that event does not inherently place a child on a path to self-destruction. For those instances where a child has experienced trauma, there is nevertheless a possibility for post-traumatic growth. As is implied in the name, children are able to identify positive characteristics that emerge from their grief and life after trauma. I like to think of this as meaning making, which is a prevalent component of grief. Perhaps children are able to see in themselves the ways in which they are resilient and able to overcome obstacles. They may also be able to identify those people who love them and support them, providing them with a sense of safety and the ability to have future-oriented hopes and goals. These may include an investment in loving relationships and a desire to want to influence their community or make the world a better place for others. Similarly, they may be able to reflect on their life, as it is after the death, and name positive characteristics or relationships that they attribute to a "new normal," and thus find meaning in why a person died or what that death now means to them.

Children are resilient and have the ability to understand cause and effect, life and death. We are probably hardwired to understand this. Watch a child kill an ant. Watch a child bury a goldfish. Listen, truly listen, to a child's play and hear all of the exploration of death and life that comes out in play. That is a child learning and doing his or her grief work.

"Inappropriate" Grief

I received a phone call from a mom following a difficult spring in which two teens from her town had died from suicide and another had been hit by a truck. She was calling out of concern for all the kids in town, including her sixteen-year-old daughter. She was worried that the kids were not talking about these deaths, and she wanted to be the one to catapult them into deep and rich conversation about their feelings, assuming such an outcome were even plausible, especially when forced on teens by their parents.

As she explained her concerns to me—concerns that genuinely seemed rooted in her profound sense of compassion and care—she told me about the boy who had been hit by a truck. This mom talked about the wake, where she thought an urn and the family would be at the front of the room. She was horrified to see an open casket and "appalled" that teens and ten-year-olds were kneeling around the boy's distorted body. This mom thought it was "too much" and a bad decision on the family's part. She went on to say that she was worried that all the kids who had attended the wake had been traumatized as a result.

Interestingly, she also talked about the many funerals she had attended recently, noting how bizarre it was that parents did not bring their kids to funerals anymore. "How else are they going to learn? How will they respond when it is a close loss and they've never been to a funeral?" I thought that observation made a lot of sense. Absolutely, how will kids learn about our rituals if we keep them secret? But why was she so appalled by the teenage boy who had been hit by a truck? Because he did not look like himself? I've never seen a dead person look like himself or herself.

As a culture we create ideas about appropriateness. There are not any "appropriate police" flashing their badges. There is not a funeral etiquette guidebook to help a grieving parent discern whether an open casket is "in good taste" for the guests. I have never attended a funeral with a comment box that allows guests to provide feedback to the family in case tragedy strikes again.

Dear John,

Sorry for your loss, but I found the flowers and open casket to be tacky and insensitive choices. Next time, consider a blue suit, or call me for suggestions.

Best to you and Gail!

Yet, many adults walk around with some headstrong opinions about what they think is appropriate. This same mom who was bothered by the teen's wake went on to say that she thought his younger brother was "a time bomb." She told me, "He doesn't talk about it, he walks around like everything is fine, and he is just acting like everything is OK." In her opinion about how grief was supposed to look, he was a time bomb, and she wanted to save him through a collaborated effort of parents holding vigils and forcing the teens in town to engage in discussion about the three recent deaths by talking about them on adult terms. Ideas like these are the result of caring adults who want to take charge, and they show why grief competency is so important. The following chapters will provide tools for better understanding a grieving child and not viewing him or her as a "time bomb."

The many myths and ideas that surround grief, especially children's grief, get in the way of our ability to support the bereaved and their ability to feel supported among all the muck we have created. An adult who is competent about grief can change the outcome of a tragedy and help our society reengage a defining human experience.

Components of a Child's Grief

*Time goes on, and your life is still there, and you have to live it.
After a while you remember the good things more often
than the bad. Then, gradually, the empty silent parts
of you fill up with sounds of talking and laughter again,
and the jagged edges of sadness are softened by memories.
Nothing will be the same, ever. . . . But there's a
wild world waiting, still, and there are good things in it.*
—Lois Lowry

New Year's Eve of 2005 was unforgettable. Forty-six-year-old Jim had been feeling unwell for a couple weeks, and when New Year's Eve arrived, he bowed out of the usual festivities, sending his worried wife and thirteen-year-old daughter to a family party where they would ring in the new year without him. A few days later, Jim went to the hospital and learned that he had a rare form of cancer. His bile duct was diseased, and in a short period of time the cancer would spread to his abdominal lining, killing him in less than six months.

Jim, who had been a bank executive in Alabama, had been relocated to Atlanta because of a bank merger. He and his wife, Liz, rehabbed a lovely home, enrolled their daughter in a new school, and planned their future together. Their second Christmas together in their new house would be their last, as after a few terrible months of chemotherapy and surgery, Jim found himself in a hospital bed, saying good-bye to his friends, his family, and his only child, thirteen-year-old Cooper. As his wife and daughter interred his ashes in their church memorial garden that May, they were burying a father, a husband, a lover, and a sole provider. Their lives were disrupted in a tremendous way, and the impact of Jim's death was extraordinary.

Jim's death, however, was not a singular event in time. His death was and is an event that repeats itself in his absence. His life ended in a moment, but that moment repeats itself—at first on a daily basis—throughout the lives of loved ones as they celebrate and grieve new losses and life experiences such as graduations, weddings, births, and deaths. Jim's death is all at once part of the past, present, and future.

Nor is his death an emotional event only. As Phyllis Silverman noted in the Harvard Child Bereavement Study, the social, economic, spiritual, physical, and emotional consequences continue to be felt for those who knew and remember the deceased.[1]

When Jim died, his friends, family, colleagues, church members, and neighbors came to the funeral. Though many of these relationships and networks were sustained long after the memorial service, inevitably some of these social bonds weakened in Jim's absence. After Jim died, Liz managed to keep the house for several years so that Cooper could continue her education without too much disruption, but eventually she had to move from the home she had restored with Jim to a more affordable community. Since Jim had provided the family's only income, in time Liz returned to teaching, the profession she had left in order to have her daughter.

Jim's death was also a physical and spiritual event. The once-healthy body that had required round-the-clock care as his cancer treatments took a greater and greater toll was now gone altogether. During cremation, heat consumed his body, and his ashes were buried at the church. Along with his body went his laugh, his outsized personality and jocular wit, his financial acumen, and his house handiness. The implications of his death were also spiritual because they begged the questions of *how* and *why* does a forty-nine-year-old die and leave his family behind. For his churchgoing family, Jim's death forced the question of why God would allow a father and husband to die a premature death. What was the meaning of Jim's death? Could it have been prevented? Was there someone to blame? Where could Liz and Cooper go from there emotionally, financially, socially, physically, and spiritually?

Each element or aspect of Jim's death makes up the whole. In other words, death is not simply the end of a life, and grief is not limited to the feelings that accompany that singular event. Grief is layered and complex. Each bereaved individual arrives at different conclusions. Even in households where multiple children have had the same upbringing; grieve the same person; and experience the same consequences of the societal, spiritual, and economic elements, each one's grief is unique. Each child interprets, perceives, and experiences different feelings that aid her in her grief and enable her to construct an individual grief story. Eventually, each child will develop a unique and special narrative to tell through her eyes and feelings.

There are a million ways in which other people and variables affect a child's grief story. In order to better understand and witness the grief story of children like Cooper (which we agree is a nonlinear narrative unique to each child and without stages or a timeline), let's explore some common processes in the grief experience.

Like many of my colleagues, I believe that there are three core processes to children's grief. These processes should not be understood as sequential or transitive, but as fluid, connected, intermittent, and possibly concurrent. A grieving child seeks to:

1. Understand that the person has died or that death has happened

2. Feel his or her feelings

3. Continue loving and trusting in other people and relationships[2]

If we use these three processes as a framework for how to think about the grief stories of children, we must work to understand the many factors that aid or interfere with a child's full exploration of his or her grief. The factors can vary depending on the way someone died, whether it was a public or private event. Cooper's grief occurred in a private forum within the intimate space of her family and friends. Let's compare her private development of coping skills with another child's public grief by looking at a tragedy like 9/11.

In anticipation of the tenth anniversary of the September 11 terrorist attacks, I spoke with CNN about parenting while grieving. Since 9/11, many bereaved families affected by the attack have done some courageous work, despite the challenges they face as individuals who grieve loved ones who died in the most public of tragedies. As I got to know some of the 9/11 families who came to Good Grief, I began to see how an event I had previously known only from a distance was a tragedy full of different perspectives and complex stories, each one replete with individual and communal implications. For example, many grieving kids who want to talk about their dads who died on 9/11 are interrupted by those who want to share their own 9/11 stories, even if theirs are about where they were that morning watching the news. It can be tricky to honor the second set of stories while remaining present to and supportive of the first.

Several women who lost their husbands in 9/11 work at or are affiliated with Good Grief, and I greatly admire each of them. From my perspective, 9/11 was the first time in ages, if ever, that Americans acknowledged children's grief in a public way. So many young parents died on that day, leaving behind teens, young children, toddlers, and infants. After 9/11, a lot of resources were contributed to the families. As a result, these kids had access to grief camps, therapy, support groups, and other bereavement networks in an unprecedented way. Their grief is unique because the death of their parents and other loved ones occurred in front of the world, politicians, commentators, neighbors, friends, and family.

How did the children who experienced the death of a parent on 9/11 come to understand the death? What does their experience teach us about a framework for children's grief?

Many of these children were accustomed to having a parent who frequently went on international business trips, as that was the way of life for many professionals who worked in the Twin Towers. The kids were used to not seeing a parent for one to three weeks, as bedtime schedules and business trips conflicted with each other. Understanding that context, we witnessed the grief stories of children who, by and large, did not immediately see the body of the person who had died, and others whose parents were returned in fragments multiple times over many months or years. How does a child understand the loss of a complete relationship with a parent when the child only sees a femur shard, finger fragment, or pelvis brought home over time? How does a child understand a death that, at least initially, might feel like an absence from an extralong business trip?

We should be careful not to say that these experiences are bad or traumatic for the children of 9/11, as such a judgment devalues the absolutely unique kind of suffering that those events imposed. Each child perceives the death, the cause of death, and his or her future differently. Rather than assume that all the children affected by 9/11 reacted uniformly, caregivers should witness and be conscious of the particularities of each child's grief story.

What are the similarities between the children of September 11 and thirteen-year-old Cooper? What are the differences? Cooper was at her father's bedside at 5:15 a.m. when he breathed his final breath. She placed his urn into the earth and was a part of each ritual from the good-bye to the interment. She saw and felt death. When Mike, the dad of eight-year-old Kelly, died in the south tower, she didn't see her father dead. Mike's body didn't return home.

What feelings comprised Cooper's and Kelly's grief as they each tried to understand that their dads were dead and physically gone forever? And how did they rebuild their complex lives and an understanding of the world so that they would both one day move away for college, leaving their moms behind, while having faith in God and love for life?

Cooper and Kelly had to work through their thoughts and feelings, finding ways to recommit to living and to future relationships. Both had to understand the events as finite and reenvision their lives without their fathers (possibly arriving at multiple versions of that vision over time, some hopeful and some bleak); both had to reshape their worldview to account for and understand the death. Both felt a need to care for their moms, and both had to feel their own feelings. Feelings come in many varieties, and if we allow children to feel and experience all their feelings (even socially unacceptable feelings), such as anger, disbelief, joy, relief, indifference, and every other emotion, we empower their grief and honor their experience. In their own way and at their own pace, because their grief stories were respected, Cooper and Kelly were both able to understand that their dads had died, and that they could live and experience happiness again despite their dads' deaths.

Honoring All Feelings

A teenage boy recently shared a journal entry with me. He wrote:

My father died in August. Lately I feel, for lack of a better word, confused. My thoughts are choppy; my mind seems to be constantly running through my thoughts, yet they always seem to stop abruptly. I am able to relay this back to you because of the continuing pattern. Headaches seem to come more often, and I feel as if my mind itself is struggling. I remember the way I felt four days after his passing when all the company had paid their respects.

I was angry. So angry, not at my father but at my family. They teased me about a few things and for some reason this anger exploded within me. I never felt this way before, so consumed by anger that it engulfed my entire being.

In a similar fashion, nine-year-old Callie exclaimed, "I don't have a dad!" Everyone took a step back, not knowing what to say to Callie, as she insisted that her dad wasn't in heaven. He was dead, and she was sick of adults telling her that it was going to be OK. In Callie's world, she felt abandoned and alone, completely alienated by adults who thought they were saying helpful things. She was even growing frustrated with her Good Grief peers, who were repeating the same grief rhetoric that she hated hearing from the adults.

Callie was mad. She was furious. Her best friend had been taken away from her when her dad had died in his sleep. He had been her cuddle buddy, her ski partner, her playmate, and her confidant. Her world centered on her dad, and in his absence she was left to be "pissed off" at the world. Callie's strong feelings made a lot of adults uncomfortable. Callie didn't care, though. She knew she was justified and wasn't concerned whether the adults in her life could manage her anger.

I knew Callie for three years. The anger didn't ruin her or alienate those who took the time to understand or affirm her. She was a great kid, even with her anger and sadness. Soon after her dad died, Callie was able to identify the adults in her life who respected her and her process. When she struggled in school and was having a hard day, she knew which adults to seek out, and they quickly became her advocates. When someone wasn't helpful, at first she told the person so; but that led to unpleasant consequences like detentions and verbal lashings. She soon learned to nod and suppress all her feelings by being a so-called good and compliant child. Those adults may have thought they were having a positive impact on her, but chances are she just changed her expectations of them and waited for the conversation or intervention to conclude, knowing that they weren't going to meet or respect her needs. Kids are smart like that!

Callie's anger was appropriate, normal, and completely natural. Not only was it a normal reaction, but also one that served a purpose. That's where she needed to be in her feelings process. The wide spectrum of feelings is available to children in the same way that it is available to adults. How feelings get expressed or articulated may look different, but each feeling has a purpose and value for the process. Caring adults can help these feelings come out in a healthy way, or we can simply get in the way.

Sam died in the spring of 2008. He was thirteen years old and the big brother of his two sisters, who were seven and eleven at the time. Sam had an undiagnosed disease, and when he died in the middle of the night, his family was devastated. How do you begin to understand that your big brother died in his sleep? What feelings accompany such a tremendous event in the life of your family?

I've known Sam's family for almost five years, and theirs is a story of hope, resiliency, and rebirth. Sam, according to his doting sisters, was the best big brother ever. Their memory of him is one that revolves around theater. He loved to act, and taught his sisters how to perform. They now share a love for the art. Both Casey and Vicki have had lead roles in their school musicals and take tremendous pride in an art that brings them closer to Sam every time the curtain opens and the orchestra begins. Although Casey and Vicki's parents, their household, and their lives dramatically changed, how have they both found ways to go on living and loving? Where do kids find such courage? How do they trust and invest in relationships now that they know any one of their lives could end in the middle of the night?

The fragility of life is not lost on children. The impermanence and vulnerability of the human experience is not a secret shared only with adults. Kids know. Kids know that those they love will die, and they know they, too, will die. Why, then, in attempting to shelter them from death, do we so consistently get in the way of children as they develop the coping skills and resiliency necessary to grieve and make healthy choices? Why do we tell our kids death will not happen to us, instead of honoring their fears when they ask us if we will die?

Can each of these processes—thinking, feeling, and loving—occur on its own in the rich inner lives of children? I think so. Can these processes be enhanced and made more solid with the help of others? Absolutely.

Facilitating the Grief Process

We can help children grieve by facilitating the process. The word *facilitate* literally means "to make easy." How do we make the grieving process easier? Support, love, listening, compassion, empowerment, and patience are some of the things at the core of supporting a grieving child.

In order to learn the ways in which we can facilitate grief, it is important to have an understanding of those variables that impede the process. I think each these three variables has a history and context that affects a child's grief, often without adults or the child being aware of it:

1. Culture

2. Religion

3. Socioeconomic status

America is rich with diverse cultural perspectives and practices. As an Irish-Italian Catholic, I was raised in a culture that had strong ideas about right and wrong; guilt and responsibility; justice and redemption. My family culture is full of saints and sinners, graphic images of suffering, religious ritual, and familial celebration and feasting. These characteristics affected how I expressed my grief as a teenager. When family members died, I created many private rituals in my bedroom as I tried to honor them, because I came from a culture that placed a high value on ritual. Despite the prevalence of rituals within my religious upbringing and within my family dynamic, I didn't witness the adults talking about the dead or performing rituals after a certain period of time—a time frame arbitrarily shaped and defined by a culture that made adults feel ashamed when they exceeded the timeline. So I noticed that the rituals were withdrawn, and I understood there was something shameful about them. As a result, I chose to do them in private, and I stashed mementos that reminded me of the dead or collected relics from their possessions (some that had been given to me and some that I stole because I was ashamed to ask for them). Theology and ideology also accompanied the rituals.

The Impact of Religious Beliefs on Understanding Grief

On the last day of his life, my Uncle Anthony visited my grandmother for chicken soup. She told him that his haircut looked handsome, and she hoped he would have a fun evening with his grandchildren—a newborn, a four-year-old, and a six-year-old. He had a lovely time, visiting La Salette Shrine in Attleboro, Massachusetts, where trees and manger scenes were covered with hundreds of thousands of Christmas lights. Anthony and the grandkids drank hot chocolate and lit a candle in memory of my grandfather.

An hour after sipping hot chocolate, he was a block from his son's house. The grandkids were in the backseat on their way to be dropped off. Anthony looked at his wife and said that he felt dizzy. Immediately, he pulled the car into a pizza shop and put it in park. And just as quickly as he was able to stop, he was gone. His son ran to the scene and tried to resuscitate him. A pizza shop employee took the kids inside and fed them while first responders used a defibrillator and rushed Anthony to a hospital. But he was gone.

A few days later, I was sitting in a packed church and a very sweet and pastoral priest was telling us that Anthony's death was part of God's plan. Anthony's work was done, he said. It was well-intentioned but watered-down theology that he hoped would help my family—my aunt, cousins, father, and grandmother—feel held by a God who knows exactly what God is doing, giving us permission to surrender our feelings, doubts, and pain to the master plan.

While we were sitting in that church, a gunman killed children and adults in Newtown, Connecticut, just two hours away. While my grandmother wailed at the grave of her oldest son, the country was learning about this tragedy, and parents everywhere joined in the deep belly grunts and wails that are raw grief. In such moments of vulnerability, uncertainty, and pain, we ask, "Where is God?" or, "How does God let these things happen?"

Caregivers, educators, clergy, and friends have to ask themselves if they want to be of use to the grieving. If so, we must be willing to stand in the shadows and live with the mystery and uncertainty of death and tragedy. Those who come forward ready to shout and proclaim God's goodness or claim to have seen the Architect's master plan will often find themselves preaching their own comforts rather than hearing and witnessing God's mysterious presence in those experiencing profound pain.

I believe God is love. I have witnessed God's presence a thousand times, and it is in those moments that I am most moved. Fred Rogers's mother said that when horrible things happen, look for all the people in the crowd doing good for one another. There, that's where I see God. Of course, each of us has our own theology or perspective, and if we are not willing to put ours to rest so that someone else's may emerge, then our effectiveness will be limited.

A few days after my uncle died, my cousin and I were chatting. He is the one who tried to revive his dad to no avail. He said, "I'm a scientist. I don't believe the stuff we were brought up with as kids. I have big questions." Me, too. I did not need to use his vulnerability to help him see or believe in God. Those questions are important and serve a purpose. When the priest preached, I had my eyes on my cousins to watch their reactions. Was Anthony's work done? He would have retired in five years or less. His newborn granddaughter had yet to be spoiled and adored like her cousins. Anthony's work was not done. I can testify to that. So why do those of us who claim to know God fill the air with ideas that are unhelpful? Why do we put out ideas that do not reflect the unfathomable mysteries of God and life? Why do we reach for pat answers when we are faced with the mystery of death?

Slain children are not a part of God's plan, I would suspect. I wonder what the clergy said to those packed churches after that school shooting in Connecticut. When we tell children that someone's death is a part of God's plan (please keep in mind that there are many ways for someone to die, for example, homicide, suicide, school shootings, and so on) they wonder why God would do such a thing, particularly to them. Why would God take *my* daddy? When we tell children that God needed another angel, children want to know why God doesn't share. "That's not fair," they will rightly say. When we project our own theologies onto children, utilizing their grief as a chance to help them understand the world as we do, we are simply capitalizing on their vulnerability. We are failing to provide them with tools to help them cope for the rest of their lives.

When I am with children, I'm never interested in telling them what I believe. I'm there to support them. I want to understand what they believe and the conclusions they are making. If I am approached to explore their feelings and ideas with them, I walk very lightly so that my agenda does not impair their grief work, their exploration of finding God and love.

When I listen to the story of my Uncle Anthony's death, I see God in the love his son offered as he tried to save him. I see God in Anthony's last days, because he had a chance to see his friends and his mother, and be with his wife and grandchildren. I see love in those moments and in all the people who offered the family support. *I* see it. I do not need to force others to see it in order to feel like I'm being helpful.

When children are slain in their classroom, it is hard to see God. But I see God in all the heroic moments, in the support that was offered to families and the community. I see love, and I have no need to force others to see it with me.

65

For many people in grief, God-talk can be very challenging as they grapple with questions of "how" and "why." Being able to walk in the mystery and uncertainty is the truest testament of faith, in my opinion. Surrendering to the unknown is a lot more difficult than surrendering to a master plan. When speaking with children, we often have to embrace the mystery, offer love and compassion, and stick with the basics. We don't have to answer the "why" and "how" for children, but we can assure our children that God is with us as we suffer. We can do so by doing good for others and pointing out all of those moments when someone has done something good for us. I believe that most of the time that's as far as we will get, and that is OK.

Religion Can't Fill in All the Blanks

When I was twelve, a childhood friend named Jimmy died from suicide after committing an embarrassing act that had made him a taunted figure in his town. I worried about him going to hell, because a priest had told me that people who killed themselves went to hell for disrespecting the life God had given them. I worried terribly about Jimmy for many years. He had been so kind to me as well as my cousins, who had played with him regularly. He didn't deserve hell, and I certainly didn't come up with the idea of punishment and hell. My religion told me that. I'm not sure I would have ever confused suffering for selfishness or disrespect on my own, at least not in my adolescent understanding of life and hurt. I was more interested in knowing and understanding why he had taken his own life than I was in the consequences of that action on an afterlife. However, adults have a lot to say about the afterlife—whether or not it exists, and especially who will be punished or rewarded.

The afterlife and its accompanying theologies are often utilized as a means to teach a child about "where Mommy is," now that the child can no longer see or touch Mommy. Though a child might express apparent understanding of an afterlife by repeating the idea of heaven and hell, children do not use abstract ideas to wrestle with difficult experiences in the same way that adults do. Rather, an abstraction like the afterlife, while seeming to comfort, can in fact confuse and frustrate a child's grief processes.

Religion often teaches a prescribed belief that explains why suffering exists or why terrible things happen to good people. The Calvinistic idea that "it is part of God's plan" is one of many mantras that are spoken to kids. This lens can shape how children understand their grief or the loss they have experienced. And it certainly shapes their ideas about God. I've heard many kids say, "Well, why can't God share Mommy with me? Why does he keep her all to himself?" I am often amazed at how theological ideas intended to reassure children of God's presence can end up exacerbating alienation and doubt.

Many times, religious teachings or inherited belief systems don't explain children's questions or meet their needs for understanding. Religion may have been a huge part of their lives previously, but now religion is banished from their daily lives as they feel victimized by a supposedly loving God who appears to have failed them. It's as if to say, "If God loves me so much, then, how did God let this happen to me—and to my wonderful daddy, of all people?" These powerful feelings present immediate challenges to the emerging worldviews of many grieving kids. In such times of spiritual crisis or discernment, a child may find it impossible to continue on with inherited beliefs that do not leave room for mystery or uncertainty. In a similar fashion, the metaphors and metaphysical concepts that comprise many religions can confuse a child, depending on where he or she is developmentally, because the boundary between concrete and abstract thinking is not crossed until early adolescence. What adults would consider useful abstractions often translate for younger children into magical thinking.

Metaphors and the Mess They Make

A few years back, I received a call from a dad who was worried about his two children, who were five and seven at the time. His wife had died in a car accident the morning before. After he received word of her death, he collected himself, made a few calls, and then contacted the school. He drove himself to the school, where his children were waiting for him out front. Naturally, he wasn't sure what to say or how to say it. He was distraught and grasping for answers as he tried to do the right thing for his kids. When he arrived at the school, he got out of his car and approached his children, who were standing next to a counselor.

As Dad approached the kids, he knelt down and said to them, "Mommy died this morning in an accident. The angels came and took her to God in heaven. I love you so much, and I'm so sorry." The children sensed his fear and pain, and they cried with him. The three of them returned home, where Dad made funeral arrangements, notified friends and family, and did all he could to support the children.

The following day, Dad and the kids needed to leave the house. However, the kids were hysterical. This surprised him because they had seemed to be "taking it well." Whenever there was mention of leaving the house, the kids freaked out. Someone helped this dad ask the children a few basic questions in order to better understand why they were upset and to determine if it had to do with Mommy. Were they afraid that they'd get into an accident, too? What was it that they found so upsetting?

The kids told Dad that they were afraid angels were going to take them away. Imagine Dad's surprise when he realized that the metaphor he had used was causing his children to be terrified that a flock of angels was going to swoop down and take them away to God in heaven.

When Dad called, he was tearful, worried that his words had made an awful event all the worse and that their chances of having a normal life were now completely obliterated. I helped Dad back-pedal. "You did not break anything. You've done nothing that you can't undo. It's OK." Dad explained to the kids that he was so sad, and he hadn't known what to say to them. He then explained death in a matter-of-fact and biological way. For the time being, he left religion, metaphors, and clichés out of the narrative and worked with the basics. The kids could understand the basics, and soon thereafter the fear of angels taking them away dissipated.

Our spiritual beliefs are often very helpful to us and are how we understand death and suffering. However, spiritual beliefs also tend to be very sophisticated and abstract, making them unclear and confusing for a child who is primarily concerned with the here and now, what can be seen and heard. Every parent, it is hoped, knows his or her child and can assess the child's ability to comprehend ideas or beliefs. I believe those religious parents who are most successful in supporting their children lead with the facts and supplement with religion where and when appropriate. Sometimes, it is appropriate to wait a few years and facilitate a child's understanding of the events instead of interjecting religious ideas that can be hard to understand or leave little room for exploration. For example, a friend of mine, who is also a minister, told me how he had explained his grandmother's death to his children. At the time, he told his three-year-old that Grammy was in heaven with Jesus. His daughter was fine with this information. However, a few days later, when they were at the cemetery for the interment, she kept staring at the casket and looking around, totally distracted during the ritual. Eventually, she piped up, "Daddy, if Grammy is in heaven, who is in the box?" Well, Grammy is in heaven, and she certainly can't be in two places at once. So is she in heaven or in the casket? Euphemisms and metaphors are hard for children to understand, even if the adults in their lives believe them or find them comforting.

Abstract religious ideas are not the only thing that can be confusing for a child. Culture is also confusing for children, who may not know the history and context even as they face communal responses that may not mirror their individual experiences. For example, there are complex culturally conditioned responses to suicide that can confuse a child who loses a loved one in this way. Although religious ideas about suicide influence American culture, the culture at large has created an attitude toward suicide that transcends religion. Whatever theological beliefs may have historically shaped our thinking about suicide in the United States, we now have a dominant cultural attitude toward suicide that embraces fears that public acknowledgment will cause contagion as well as stigmas surrounding the person who died and stigmas surrounding the family. Blame, evasion, discomfort, and shame are frequently visited upon the family.

American culture, by and large, interprets suicide as a selfish and criminal act. Consider the language we have for this type of death. For example, people "commit suicide." What other types of things do people commit? Murder. Crime. Felony. Treason. Adultery. Even the word itself—*suicide*—literally means "self murder," in the same way that *homicide* means "the murder of another human." The way we talk about suicide is inherently loaded with baggage and judgment. We call people who take their lives "selfish" or "cowards." I imagine it would take a lot of guts to look down the barrel of a gun and not flinch, yet we call these people "weak." These cultural stigmas and ideas don't mirror the reality of the situation or death.

I have worked with dozens of kids who are survivors of a loved one's suicide, many of whom found their loved ones after the death. The majority of these kids struggle immensely to understand why their mother or brother did it. A child may naturally feel victimized by the event, wondering if Dad didn't love her enough to stay alive, or asking, "Did Dad do this to hurt me?" Expressed cultural attitudes that suicide is shameful or selfish can compound a child's normal feelings of resentfulness and make it harder for her to know and have compassion for the psychological suffering her father experienced before his death. However, I have also worked with many children who understand exactly why the death happened because they had witnessed their love one's profound sadness and pain for months or years leading up to it. The compassion these kids have for their deceased family member is deeply moving and an example of the positive attributes a grieving child can develop.

When it comes to homicide, prevailing news and entertainment narratives more often than not link murder victims (and their murderers) to cultures of criminality and violence. Frequently this linkage is tied up with assumptions about the racial identities and socioeconomic statuses of those involved. These assumptions saturate our culture: think of how many crime procedural television shows airing during prime time depend on a murder for entertainment. However, when supporting an individual grieving child who has a unique grief story, the stories our culture tells about homicide—often to entertain or sensationalize us—can obstruct with gross assumptions our ability to be present and to respond to that child's needs and process.

Our Deaths Do Not Define Us

Similarly damaging narratives can surround common diseases. People who die of lung cancer deserved it because they smoked. People who die of heart disease should have dieted. Those who overdose were reckless addicts and their lives had no value. If you don't believe these are commonly held beliefs, then tell someone your dad died of lung cancer. Wait thirty seconds to see if he or she asks whether your dad smoked. I bet you get that question before you finish your sentence. In each of these cases, the cultural assumption can prevent those who care for a grieving child from asking about and getting to know the real person who died, who of course was so much more—and more complicated—than just "an addict" or "a smoker." We are more than the cause of our deaths.

We create a culture around death and dying not only by our commonly held beliefs and the way we propagate them in media and movies, but also by the probing questions we ask a family or a child. The teenager will be asked if her father smoked and, because she has learned in school that smoking kills, she'll know that the person asking the question is finding blame. That affects a child's grief. And where it is true, I've heard many kids ask, "Why did he smoke when I asked him to stop? Did he not love me?" We reinforce these beliefs and feelings when we create a culture of blame and insist on cause-and-effect justifications to ease our own coping.

We are a culture that puts a lot of responsibility on the individual. We like to hold people accountable on all sorts of fronts. That spills over into how we understand why bad things happen. Therese was killed in a car crash. Well, was she speeding or texting? Eric fell off the roof. Why wasn't he wearing a harness? Peter died of liver failure. Drunk! A child's understanding of death is shaped by what his community has to say about it, but also by what the community is *not* saying or how the community creates secrets around some events. This includes schools that banish the mention of students who have died from suicide.

The degree to which communal beliefs influence a child can also depend on the child's socioeconomic status. Socioeconomic status includes not only financial resources and income, but also occupation, education, region, community type (rural, urban, or suburban), and health. Socioeconomics shape values and ideas about grief. A child's socioeconomic status will affect his or her support systems, access to resources, and ability or willingness to seek help if it is needed. Few people in the United States have access to local support, such as Good Grief. In both rural and densely populated communities, many children grieve alone. The majority of the population, including skilled professionals, is not educated about grief, allowing stigmas and misunderstandings to permeate our communities.

When I think about the many variables that impede a child's grief, I often have two reactions. The first is admittedly juvenile and laced with curse words, as I blame adults for making it all the more difficult for kids. After coming up with some creative names to accompany my frustrations, I eventually remember that simply being able to name these impediments is a good thing. It gives us direction.

There is nothing lovely or delightful about the insensitivities that cultural assumptions visit on grieving kids. But they are just that: *communal assumptions*. They aren't permanent and they aren't authoritative, although they can feel like it to children. Community contextual factors that interfere with children's grief processes are not a terminal disease. Any of these variables can evolve and change if we engage them honestly. The more we become aware of our impact on children, the more we can be intentional about what we know, what we merely assume, how we interact or avoid interacting, and ultimately, how we support a grieving child.

So yes, there is a lot of cultural, religious, and socioeconomic baggage facing a grieving child. But it doesn't have to be this way, and it won't be this way forever as communities rally around grieving families, remove impediments, and work to create healthier, more supportive responses to death. As we continue to evolve and grow, we will arrive at a time when we can acknowledge and honor the unique grief story of each child.

Respecting a Child's Grief Work

Honoring is a big word for a child. However, it's not so big that the concept cannot be understood. In fact, its magnitude is felt when it is present in the life of a child. How many children are truly hon-ored for who they are and how they understand the world in their own mystical, magical way? And how many narratives spoken by a child are honored for what they are and what they mean to the child? The child who is indifferent to the death; the child who wants to believe his dad was Superman; the child who didn't like the parent as much as you did; the child whose story doesn't mirror your reality but hers—each of these experiences is valid, and we need to respect the individual experience.

What about the child who expresses feelings or ideas that makes us uncomfortable? How do we honor that child's grief expression? When we honor a grieving child's story, we provide him or her a place and all the time in the world to mourn.

Alan comes to Good Grief because his brother died on the train tracks. His feelings about his brother may be similar or identical to some of his peers' feelings about their dead siblings. However, his relationship with his brother was like no one else's. It was not a magical relationship that had qualities that no other fraternal relationship ever possessed. It wasn't so unique that *National Geographic* followed them their entire lives. It wasn't so unique that no one else could ever possibly relate.

But it was unique because all relationships are unique. Its many parts may look like any other sibling relationship, but the feelings, stories, and shared experiences make up the whole. It's that whole and the ways in which *Alan* feels, experiences, and interprets the whole that make it unique. The same is true for how he feels, experiences, and interprets his brother's death. And it is unique despite the many external variables that affect his story and attempt to force it into a prescribed narrative.

However Alan feels about his brother's death and their relation-ship is OK. As we honor his story, we help Alan make sense of the parts. The narrative may be one of profound love that evolves into a hint of resentment. Or perhaps they disliked each other, but in his brother's absence Alan begins to develop affection for his brother.

The story evolves. The relationship evolves. The life has ended, but the relationship doesn't.

Lives End but Relationships Continue

I believe this view of death, in which we allow our feelings about and relationships with the dead to change long after the death itself, is a needed shift in how we think about the dead and talk about them with children. To adopt this perspective would also say a lot about how we want to live our lives and influence those important relationships and people in our lives.

What we say to our children contributes to their lifelong inner voice. The ways in which we love and the ways in which we neglect one another don't end when the heart-rate monitor flatlines and announces our death to those in the room. They don't end when the obituary goes live on the local news website. They don't end when our bodies turn to earth. Our words and actions carry on in our absence, and they do so without room for remediation. There is no time for amendments or heartfelt apologies.

Lives end but relationships continue. The people who go on living have the greatest role in determining what that relationship looks like. Do they cut the dead completely out of their lives? Do they visit and bring flowers? Do they do the things they loved to do together? Do they eat the person's favorite food to remember? Do they stop and think about the person or feel love as the person's name is spoken or a story is shared? The relationship continues.

Many bereaved children remain in lifelong relationship with those who died. They may need to work through their feelings, which may include forgiveness, resentment, happiness and joy, or sadness that accompanies their grief. The inner voice that children absorb from adults, from praise to judgment, shapes who the children become; sometimes kids know it is there and can embrace it, and sometimes they need to overcome it. But it sticks with them—as with all of us who once were children—long after the loved one dies.

A Dialogue without Words

At the end of the day, death is a dialogue without words in that we remain in communication about and with the dead for as long as it is important for us to do so. This one-way communication infuses the past relationship with ongoing feelings and desires.

The evolution of a child's ongoing relationship with the dead can be complex and fearful, especially when adults tell children, "You still have Daddy in your memories." Memories are intangible, and they dissolve over time. It's not helpful to put that type of pressure on a kid, as if to say, "Your daddy's immortality rests in you and your ability to remember." Yikes! Do you remember the telephone number to your childhood home? I don't; but it was the one important thing I was supposed to know in case I got lost, abducted, or had an emergency. Why should we lead children to believe that the only way to access the dead is through memory? When the memories fade, is that the end of the relationship? The end of the dead? The end of one's youth? Many children fear forgetting, so it can be helpful to make some memories concrete.

At Good Grief we have a special room called the Memory Box Vault. Inside, it is full of decorated boxes that the kids have made. They are invited to put memories in the box they have made, make things for the person who died and store them in the memory box, and interact with the box however they'd like. A lot of the boxes are empty. Many kids only have a few memories of their own to place in their box. Maybe it's a baseball game or a fishing trip. Maybe it's a visit to Disneyland. We have the memory boxes available for the kids, but we don't have any expectations for those boxes because some kids have few memories of their own or only stories that others have shared.

As a result of temperamental memories, kids enjoy hearing stories about the person who died. Some kids have received stories from their parent's friends, coworkers, and relatives, and that is one way to support a child. Those narratives can be helpful to children as they grow up and piece together the story of their big brother or parent. The stories are helpful as children remain in dialogue with the dead and try to understand and know the person.

The stories of the dead may have a lot to say about a child's life, how he got here, and the story of his childhood. Children try to fit the stories of the dead into their own life story to make themselves whole. In a similar way, stories influence how a child sees himself in a larger context. The dead, for a grieving child, may help the child understand how he fits into the world. Children often fill in the blanks with imagination and wishful thinking—sometimes in a helpful way, but sometimes not. That is why it is important for caring adults to keep lines of communication open and be willing to engage the child's own self-understanding over time.

The narrative of an individual may have something to say to and about a community—just as much as communal assumptions can influence how an individual understands a death—especially if the individual story is rooted in communal tragedy. Stories of grief regarding genocide, terrorism, war, poverty, violence, refugees, and so on affect a child's understanding of herself and her people. The story is no longer about the individual alone, but also about people "like me" and others "not like me." From these experiences and the stories we create from them, children abstract notions of justice and the consequences of caring or not caring for strangers, neighbors, friends, and family.

These notions intertwine to become the fabric of the community, which, in turn, intertwines with other communities to create our broader culture. But not all is sweetness and light. Bad things happen, and sometimes children have a difficult time integrating stories and making sense of things, especially if violence is involved, creating an environment of constant anxiety. This reintroduces questions about trauma. If trauma is a self-perceived threat to one's own life, then the communal threat and the anxiety the threat spawns will affect the way a child expresses and experiences grief.

One does not have to live through the wars of Rwanda or Syria to understand the concept of justice and how it pertains to grief. There are plenty of what amount to war zones in the United States. A mother brought her four kids to Good Grief because their brother had died. His siblings, ranging from three to seventeen years old, had an understanding of justice and its consequences for those who had murdered their brother. The family was quite open about what had happened. They were from a community that had some incredibly high murder rates. This family had evidence to prove, or they believed—the difference between the two doesn't matter—that the police had killed their brother.

In a country and within a community that remained riddled with gun violence, these four children grieved their beloved brother; but there was more to their story. This boy they adored had been killed, and now each of them faced a life within a community with the same threats and risks for them. Their neighbors faced those threats. Their family faced those threats. As a result, their narrative was not only about death and grief, but also about the violence, poverty, and institutions that affected their lives.

As these kids grieved their big brother and made meaning out of his life and death, they also tried to understand how they would avoid a similar outcome for themselves. They needed to know whom they could trust. They could not trust the police. Telling these children that they could, in fact, trust the police and those men and women who had sworn to protect them would be a futile task. That had not been their experience to date. A communal narrative and the tragedies that surrounded them on a daily basis affected their grief story.

So whether the death happens in a hospital room or on the street in front of many eyes, children work to process their grief by understanding how the death happened and that the person is now dead. They work to understand the finality of death, and through that process, they find ways to express all their feelings. They have to work out what this death means to them, but also what death, itself, means. And despite the complexity and perhaps, at times, confusion that accompanies their grief, each of these children can find ways to go on living and loving.

Children are wonderfully resilient, and although they are just as susceptible to bad things as us adults, their stories are never over when tragic things happen. Their stories can be shared, and their lives can evolve in hopeful ways despite the difficulties we might wish we could prevent.

In that hope and in the unfailing resilience of children, I believe our greatest human qualities exist. From birth, we have the capacity to form new bonds and new communities, to trust again, and to have faith that we will not be alone when death returns, even for us.

Chapter 5

What Do We Tell the Children?

If only words were the antidote to cure hurt. If only superb wordsmithery could take away pain and resolve our problems or fully articulate the complexities of our emotions and desires. Language is problematic, however. It is susceptible to the tone of our delivery, to the perception of others, to a vastness of meaning or an empty void, to interpretations, and to each individual's understanding or internalization of particular words.

How do we communicate compassion? Our faith that everything will be OK? Our fear that our individual lives might be on the cusp of collapse? My understanding of anger might look very different from yours, and your interpretation of fear might look very different, in your context, compared to mine. We often act as though words are just words, but they can be loaded and layered with meaning, history, and interpretation.

Words are often what keep us apart when we grieve. We can't find the right words, so we say nothing at all. We are unsure of how to begin trudging through grief's layers of uncertainty and unpredictability, so we sit back and ponder how to approach the bereaved; and in the meantime our search for words increases their feelings of loss and isolation. Likewise, the grief of a child who appears to be "doing fine" confuses adults, who are often unsure of how to support a child who doesn't look as though she is in crisis.

Words, however, are not the only way we communicate. We communicate with our eyes, ears, body, movement, and sounds, as well as our presence or absence.

When the family I described in chapter 4—the mom and four kids—came into my office, I asked them to share their story with me. They told me that their brother had been murdered a few weeks before. They had that look in their eyes that many newly bereaved families have: deer in the headlights. They knew my name. They knew what I did and what I represented. They were looking around the room and seeing drawings that said, "I miss you, Dad," or, "I wish I could bring you back for one more Yankees game." And as this family sat in this space with me, they were probably thinking what many families articulate: *You've got to be kidding me. Am I really here? Is this really happening? This is one more surreal thing in this long nightmare.*

As the family and I talked, I heard the preteen and teens tell affectionate stories about how much they loved their big brother. He was their hero. They looked up to him in each and every way. And Mom just adored her oldest child.

Caught up in the sharing and the love, I was happy when Mom asked me if I wanted to see a photo of her son. I was expecting to see an athletic twenty-year-old, surrounded by friends, and probably hugging someone to his left and right while wearing a big grin. It just seemed like he had been that kind of kid.

Mom reached into her purse and removed the photo. It looked a little worn and must have been shown to many people over the past few weeks. As she placed it into my hand, I looked down at the five-by-seven image. There he was; but he was not being hugged, not smiling, and not at all what I expected. It was an image of him shot in the head in the front seat of his car.

As I looked at the image, I heard his mom say that this photo had been texted to her daughter two hours after the murder. I was aware that Mom and the kids were staring at me to gauge my reaction. In that moment, my eyes, my body, and my sounds were all communicating to the family.

Staring at the murdered twenty-year-old, I panicked for a moment and wondered what my face was saying. What had I done when I first processed what I was looking at? In a moment like that, there aren't right or wrong responses, but having the self-awareness to check in with myself and recall how I had responded helped me figure out what to do next.

As I recall this moment, I think my posture remained the same, my head did not go flinching back, I did not gasp, and I remained calm as I took in the intensity of the image. I responded by saying, "Oh, guys, I'm just so sorry that this happened to you and your brother. How are you doing, having received this image and having seen him like this?"

If I had jumped when I saw that photo or gasped or thrown the photo back at Mom, I might have communicated a lot of things to the family without using any words. They might have interpreted those reactions several ways:

- Their sharing of the image was bad and upsetting to me. They could have been mortified or embarrassed for having shared it.

- They may have thought that they were different, that their story was worse than others, given my terrified reaction.

- They may have felt that I didn't have the chops to be present and listen to their story.

- They may have thought their story was as bad as they believed it to be.

- The kids could have been embarrassed that Mom took out the photo again and showed their slain brother to yet another unprepared adult.

A child can develop a host of assumptions depending on how we communicate with or in front of him or her. Words are not the basis of all communication. As a result, our communication needs to be holistic and must include words, body, eyes, and presence. We must maintain what I like to call *active mindfulness.*

Mindfulness

If you have never meditated before, I highly recommend it both as a form of self-care and as a practice for how to support grieving children. Breathing in, you pay attention to your feet touching the floor, your buttocks and back touching the chair, and your head firmly rooted to your neck. Breathing out, you release the day's woes. Meditation is a practice of presence and attunement.

Of all the people I know who work with kids, the ones I admire most are those who know how to be fully in their bodies and who are also capable of getting out of them. In other words, being present with kids requires movement, such as jumping and crouching; rolling and bouncing; holding still and flailing like a dragon soaring through the clouds, stopping only to crash elegant tea parties. Simultaneously, being with kids requires adults to leave their adult ideas, insecurities, and properness at the door so that when it comes time to be the dragon or sip the imaginary tea, we can be like the kids and relate to them on their level.

I like acting like a child. It's liberating and fun; it helps me connect to the kids in a unique way. Heck, sometimes I act like a child when I'm supposed to be acting like an adult. It keeps things lively and makes the other adults think a little quicker.

Being mindful around grieving children allows them to know you are with them and meeting them where they are. It goes beyond crouching and meeting them in stature. It's also being mindful of children's needs, unpredictability, and the unique ways and times in which they may or may not express their grief. What does being mindful mean? It means keeping focused on the people you are with and not thinking about that hectic afternoon traffic or that argument you had last night. It means being aware of the other's tone, body language, words, and images.

When you think about it, being with another person can be a lot of work. But when you are with a child who says something that makes you wince or uncomfortable, being mindful also means noticing when your mind turns away into your own thoughts. When that happens, it typically means that the child's story touched a nerve in you. It can also mean that you might have issues you need to attend to in another context. As you actively listen to another, it can be helpful to picture yourself with arms wide open. But however you accomplish it, be authentic and honest. Being mindful while being with a grieving child is like saying, "I'm here. I'm fully yours. Where will you take us?" Believe me, children, can tell when you are authentically present and when you aren't. And being open breeds trust.

Most adults do not find it easy to hand over trust to a child. This is not the type of trust that allows a teen to go out with friends as long as he or she is home by 11 p.m. This is a different kind of trust, in which the adult is vulnerable to the needs of the child and arrives without expectations, being willing to participate and witness the child's grief story just by being present. It's playfulness. It's experimentation. It's a dance in which all the adults are following the child who is the lead dancer, moving from tango to swing to line dancing and finally to a little waltz.

Being mindful of our expectations, our false ideas about how the conversation is supposed to look, will shape the outcome of our efforts to support the child. Let's say we are eager to help the grieving child of a friend who recently died. If we were to invite eleven-year-old Ty to go on a day hike, we might first ask ourselves why. Why the invitation? Is it for quality time? Is it an opportunity to have fun because we enjoy hanging out? Is it a chance to get to know each other more and develop a trusting relationship? Is this an attempt to get Ty on a secluded mountain so we can ask him a million questions about his dead father, knowing Ty can't run away and will probably have to answer the questions and listen to our advice?

Being informed about children's grief and being mindful of our expectations of grieving kids, we would know that a hike would be a great opportunity for quality time and the development of trust with Ty. Maybe Ty liked to hike with his dad. Maybe they never hiked together, but Ty wished they had. He might mention that as we traverse up and down the trails.

But to think that our advice is what he needs, and probing him with questions that are invasive or that he is not ready to answer, could easily hurt that developing trust. If we are unaware of our expectations—pushing Ty to meet our own need to feel worthwhile and helpful—then when we get back to the house and collect wood for the fire to make s'mores, we will probably miss out on an intimate and authentic expression of his grief.

Rather than sharing in the silence or laughing over yet another burned marshmallow, Ty may not share how much he misses his dad or how he wishes he could spend another moment with him by the campfire. That beautiful opportunity for him to share may be lost because of our own desires to give advice, tell him how to feel, and go on a grief scavenger hunt that asks a million unwelcome questions.

Conversely, this opportunity to go for a hike with a friend's kid could be helpful if we have good self-awareness. While hiking we may hint at some of the good times we had with his dad and how much we miss him. We might mention him subtly and watch Ty to see how he responds. Is he quiet? Teary-eyed? Does he ask follow-up questions? "Oh, there we go again, Ty. We're always talking about your dad because we miss him. Are you OK if we talk about this, or would you rather talk about something else?" we might say to him. We must be mindful of his needs versus ours, while staying attuned to what his words, his body, his eyes, and his presence are telling us: follow his lead.

Follow Their Lead

I like the image of driftwood. It floats; moves around the current as it goes downstream. It gets snagged, and it breaks loose. I keep the image of driftwood in mind when grieving kids give me the runaround. When I'm baking plastic bread, killing and resurrecting teddy bears, burying toys in the sandbox, drawing images of a happy family and a sad family, or whatever I'm doing, I am drifting with the children and following their lead. They tell me where they want to go and how they want to express their grief. I simply provide some tools to help them with the process.

Many adults assume that by asking invasive questions they are being helpful. They think it shows interest and communicates an atmosphere of compassion. However, when we follow the children's lead, we become aware that kids may not be ready to talk about some things. Some feelings might feel big and scary. Some images are tucked away, and that's where they want to keep them for now. When we follow the children's lead, we believe that they are resilient and have within them the inherent ability to process the death and continue living and loving. When we follow their lead, we are led to mysterious places and to parts of their lives that we could not have imagined on our own. I show up and ring the doorbell. It's up to them to unlock the door, invite me in, and show me their world.

I don't mean to suggest that there isn't room for mentorship or guidance. However, mentors don't show up one day with all the answers. They are in dialogue and relationship, and it is through trust and mutual respect that mentors are effective. Perhaps, by following the bereaved child's lead and offering support and caring presence first, we are most able to become mentors over time, assuming the child wants to have a mentor in his or her life. A helpful mentor is first of all the dunce.

Be the Dunce

Before I worked with the dying and then the bereaved, I studied to be an archaeologist. I did my fieldwork in Belize and worked on some incredible Mayan ruins. Digging and sifting through the dirt, I uncovered stories of an ancient people. I learned about their outcasts and their poor, their riches and their religion. My archaeological hunt taught me a great deal about people who were no longer alive to tell their story.

Now, working with the grieving, I see similarities between my former profession and those who want to help grieving kids. I find that adults love their archaeological tools: trowel, Indiana Jones hat, flashlight, backpack, and all the other devices necessary to dig their way through children's lives and understand their stories or feelings.

I'm not interested in that type of grief dig. I left my archaeological tools in Belize. I don't need those tools to tell me the stories of the living. I just need to show that I care and am interested, giving them the space to tell me their stories as they choose. I would rather be the dunce than the excavator.

If I approach a conversation with a grieving child, I leave everything at the door. To the best that I can, I leave my assumptions, my judgments, my opinions, my needs, my feelings, and as much of my personal issues as possible outside the room. In other words, I walk into that interaction with only two things: the ability to be empathic and a willingness to learn. That's it. That's the spirit of my presence.

Of course, I still have some fears about how it's going to go and insecurities about tripping over my words or misunderstanding something a child is trying to tell me. That's never going to go away, but my confidence in the spirit of my presence is strong. I believe God is love. If I show up, if I'm willing to offer caring presence and nonjudgmental attentiveness, then I allow for something greater than me to have a place in the conversation: love. With love, I can just be present and wait to be led.

In walks the dunce: "Tell me." "Help me understand." "Show me." "I'm listening." With open-ended questions that invite sharing, I welcome the child to let me into his or her world. I may start off playful with a chipper "Hey you!" or "Look at those sparkly shoes you are wearing!" If I'm with an older kid, a simple "It's good to see you." Then I ask, "Tell me, what's going on?" or, "I'd love to know how you're doing. What's up?"

I think of all my interactions with kids as an invitation: I invite you to share with me. My conversation is an invitation because I frame it as such, void of probing questions, and because I show the child that he or she has my undivided attention. *I am yours,* I say to him or her with my body and my eyes and my physical movement, and I don't forget to turn off my cell phone.

If I ring the doorbell and no one answers or the child opens it for a moment and then walks away, then I'll come back in a short while or another day. I don't become insecure and take it personally, feeling badly as if I had done something wrong. Instead, I am consistent. I'll ring the bell again in a short while or at a later time.

This isn't to be confused with nagging. I'm not a nag. Nagging is annoying, it's invasive, and it's chronic. Consistency is noninvasive and as simple as being present: "I'm here. I showed up. You can talk about your grief if you want to, but you don't have to." Whereas, nagging is more like, "I'm here. I keep showing up. You can talk about your grief already because the clock is ticking." Our body language and tone of voice also differentiate nagging from consistency. Let's be honest; no one likes a nag, especially kids.

Consistency is incredibly important for grieving children. Their lives are pretty inconsistent when someone important dies. Meals may be missed or may come late at night, new faces keep showing up while old friends are nowhere to be found, and the children's routine is probably more disheveled than we can imagine. But those who are consistent and keep showing up have the opportunity to be an important person in their lives. When everyone else comes and goes, be the one always ready to chat or play. When everyone else is paying attention to Mom, be the one who sneaks out the back door to play on the swings with little Jessie. That will make a difference.

Our ability to hand over trust and let a child lead us may look like a salsa or tango or maybe the jitterbug as we are swept across the dance floor, but we are able to move and flow because we trust the process.

Trust the Process

We all agree that children don't grieve in stages, but there are some characteristics of the process—such as the thinking, feeling, and rebuilding framework that I outlined at the beginning of chapter 4—that are part of their grief story. If we know that their grief is a process, as they work through feelings, ideas, concepts, and questions we can trust that process and have faith that as long as kids are making healthy decisions, they are fine.

Trusting the process, perhaps, is one of the hardest parts of supporting bereaved children. I believe this lack of trust in their process is what is putting us on a scary path toward interventions and medical treatment for kids who are just being kids. The wrestling, the angst, and the grief bursts that are unpredictable or don't mirror adult expectations have led people who think of themselves as "helpers" to turn to medicine and treatment plans to engage and deal with an experience as normal as grief.

My trusting the process, however imperfect, has made me privy to so many beautiful stories.

Jake's mom killed herself. She had been in a great deal of pain for several years. Jake and his dad had her hospitalized for her depression, but she was so determined that she used the sheets from her bed to take her life.

Jake struggled with his mom's death throughout the four years that I knew him. He withdrew at some points; he lashed out at others; he teased and he antagonized. Perhaps that was his grief or perhaps it was his teenage moods. Jake frustrated a lot of people in these years, but we all trusted the process and met him with patience whenever we could. We stayed with him when others, such as his teachers, rejected him and cast him and his bad behavior out. We didn't make exceptions for him. We had a short list of rules that involved confidentiality, trust, respect, and giving everyone a chance to share. When he broke those rules, he was stopped. But we never abandoned him, and we showed him respect when he tried to push us away.

He worked through those feelings and he kept showing up, even though he complained. Eventually, he got his driver's license and no one could make him come to the center. However, he got in his mom's car and drove himself there week after week. He still complained, but eventually his peers laughed about it. "Jake," they said, "if you hate coming here so much then stop driving yourself here. Take a left when you're supposed to go right." They called him on it. Jake laughed, and he kept coming. His friends, people who accepted him for who he was, were at the center, and he didn't want to leave them. In fact, he loved being in their presence.

Trust the process. Let the kids work it out. At every difficult interaction and at times when I feel there is nothing more to give, I step back and think *TRUST THE PROCESS!* And the process shows me how well it's working for both of us—the kid and me!

I think it is in trusting the process that we see the humanness, the universality and purpose, of grief. In trusting the process, we see how normal and natural grief is, while also witnessing its complexities and layers. It is for this very reason that I never see a grieving child as broken or as a "time bomb." I see the potential in him or her, the courage, and the ability to learn about empathy and compassion despite the pain or challenges ahead.

In the same way, I know many adults who were grieving children. Their story is bound by their childhood grief. Some start grief centers; some try other ways to heal and make meaning. It becomes a lifelong search. Those whose grief and pain were not affirmed as children continue to carry that narrative with them well into adulthood as they search for meaning and try to find a place to pick up the process where they left off as kids. Some whose processes were interrupted or not allowed full expression turn to unhealthy coping behaviors, such as abusing alcohol and drugs and engaging in other high-risk behaviors to endure their pain.

Even so, I have witnessed so many adults share stories about their childhood grief, and their stories are stories of resiliency and phenomenal personal growth that they see in themselves. Their universal story has become one in which the process has shown them their inner strength and courage.

The process is important, and we can either support it or get in the way. I choose to support it.

As we support the process, we can think of the ways in which grief is also physiological. Children have within them the ability to grieve and process the death, but the ways in which they process it depend on where they are developmentally.

Developmental Stages

An infant grieves, a three-year-old grieves, a ten-year-old grieves, and so, too, do the teen and the young adult. But they grieve differently depending on their brains' development and limitations and the ways in which their brains process information.

I don't look at a three-year-old and make assumptions about how that child comprehends the death. That three-year-old may understand the death as well as his five-year-old sister. I like to think of the developmental stages as a guide that can help me anticipate some behaviors or things a three-year-old shares, but a child's experience, maturity, or other variables may influence the child's ability to understand and process the death.

So let's think of the developmental stages as a loose framework that provides a little direction.

Many, but not all, two- to five-year-olds engage in magical think-ing. Through that magical thinking, they may think that Mommy died because they refused to put on their shoes before going to the store. Mommy was very mad, and it's their fault that she is dead. It's as if she died to punish the child for being difficult and defiant. In the same way, the three-year-old may think that if she behaves really well, she can bring Mommy back. Being good worked with Santa and for getting all those great gifts last year, so why then couldn't it work for getting Mommy back? When their magical thinking doesn't bring Mommy back, they may become very frustrated and unable to articulate that frustration. They may even be confused. *Well, Mommy went away for a long time before; I betcha she'll be back.* "Hey, Daddy, when is Mommy coming back?"

This age group tends to love arts and crafts and play. Play is their language, and through the resurrection of dead teddy bears, elabo-rate meals prepared at toy kitchenettes, and ubiquitous scribbling, the story of their grief is revealed in spurts.

Five- to eight-year-olds are beginning to grasp language and have the ability to start articulating their feelings, frustration, and needs in a way that most adults can hear more clearly even when they aren't paying attention. This age group's Personal Death Awareness (PDA) is also increasing. "If someone important can die, so can I," or, "If Mommy can die, so can Daddy." A parent who says, "No, I'm not going to die," might as well say, "Don't worry, kid; you can't trust me. So ask me anything and I'll tell you my lies!" Kids know by this age that the surviving parent isn't invincible. And while most parents like to think that they are more important than they are, many kids just want to know who is going to feed them and take them to their friends' houses if their living parent dies. Kids at this age are still egocentric.

While assuring that their needs are going to be met, many

five- to eight-year-olds are aware of their peers. They want to be like their peers, and they feel insecure or mad when friends and loved ones don't meet their expectations. They are aware of who has been absent since Dad died.

This age group also wants to understand death in a concrete way. Abstract ideas about heaven and angels, and abstract language such as "passed away" and "in your memory," are not helpful. Kids are literal thinkers; metaphors and clichés seldom contribute much. Death is a biological function, and using straightforward language to talk about death appeals to this age group's emerging affinity for logic.

Q. How do we know we are alive?

A. We eat, drink, breathe, poop (they love that one!), burp, sleep, tweet, run, and so on.

Q. How do we know something is dead?

A. It can't eat, drink, breathe, poop, burp, sleep, tweet, run, and so on. When we die, our heart doesn't beat. Our lungs don't breathe in oxygen. Our feet can't walk, and our body no longer works.

This is concrete, biological, and straightforward. By this age, kids have also seen dead animals, have maybe experienced the death of a pet, or have another frame of reference that is a helpful tool or touch point for this conversation.

Language is incredibly important. What does it mean to "pass away"? That image reminds me of tumbleweed or a sandstorm. It's like saying, "Mom just blew away in the breeze." But she didn't. She died. Language is important for children's understanding of death, its finality, and its unpredictability, especially at this age. And honesty, of course, is crucial to children's understanding. If we clog their process with white lies, misinformation, or clichés, it will affect their processing and it may ultimately require them to regrieve with new or better information at a later date.

Some types of deaths are surrounded by more lies and half-truths than others. Suicide, for example, is a truth that tends to be shared slowly or not at all. One fall, I met with a dad whose wife had died from suicide. He had woken up in the wee hours of the morning and noticed that his wife wasn't in bed. He picked up his three-year-old son, who slept with them, and began exploring the house. He stumbled upon a note that indicated she was outside. Dad rushed out the sliding door and found her hanging on the monkey bars. The child saw her, saw his dad's reaction, and then watched Dad take her down and call 911. However, after the police came and the kids were moved to the neighbor's house for the morning, Dad told his son that what he saw hadn't happened. Dad put a different narrative in his head, but as his older sisters pried and tried to figure out what he meant when he described the rope and Daddy crying, he had to wade through a confusing narrative that contradicted what he had seen and knew.

In a similar way, some parents decide to tell white lies or half-truths to protect their children. The problem is twofold: first, people talk; second, lies not only destroy trust, they also make the grief worse. So when the child finally hears the truth—and she will—that child has all the more grief work to do as she processes why she was lied to and reimagines and regrieves the death. What adults think are helpful lies, usually cause a child to imagine something much worse than what really happened. The child will reprocess this as she gets older and matures.

Eight- to twelve-year-olds are on the cusp of their teenage years. Many are inhabiting bodies that are larger than they know how to maneuver. Hormones are beginning to increase this group's awareness of their sexual selves. This developmental stage enjoys competition and games. Some are self-conscious of their desire to play with "kid's toys" or do arts and crafts, so they might do it secretively or pretend to be disinterested. Most now have the full ability to articulate their feelings and needs with their increased command of language. Similarly, they have an increased ability for problem solving, can reason through challenges, articulate their coping skills or strategies, and even identify healthy and unhealthy coping on their own.

This age group tends to have a morbid curiosity about death, which may manifest in jokes or inquisitive questions about gory details or specifics.

Teens might be my favorite, not because they have any analytical powers that younger kids don't possess, but because I so greatly appreciate their desire for independence. Teens—kids ranging between twelve and eighteen—are becoming abstract thinkers and are full of hormones. As they develop physically, mentally, and emotionally, some parts mature faster than others, and their childlike quirks can cause their abstract-thinking minds to believe they are immortal and that the present moment is the only instant that counts. I tend to think of teens as "deep feelers," because that first love, that first disappointment, that first anything is the most important thing in the world. As a result of that characteristic, I admire the ways in which they live in the present moment. Adults, who can see that there is a long future ahead, often misunderstand that intensity of the moment.

However, when grieving teens feel isolated and alone, misunderstood and unsupported, those emotions may feel like forever. A small betrayal or disrespect may feel massive—and for them it is—and honoring that intensity is important.

I find that teens question the "how and why" of death in a big way, drawing them toward music, art, religion, and outlets that help them understand answers to their questions or ways to cope with their hurt.

Because of their emerging ability to think abstractly, teens begin to make meaning out of their grief and the death of someone important. They may find ideas about heaven, hell, and God foolish, dismissing adult theology and ideology in their entirety. This scares many adults, but it is an important part of the process because teens are trying to come up with their own framework for how the world works.

Many teens are not looking for independence from a parent just so they can drive the car wherever they want or hang out with whomever they choose. They are looking for ideological independence, too. That can include feelings about the person who died, ideas about why the person died, and thoughts about the character of the deceased. The latter can be difficult for a family when the teen doesn't think Dad was as awesome as Mom thinks he was, or vice versa.

These characteristics of grieving children's developmental abilities are just a few of the ways in which kids are capable or incapable of keeping up with adult expectations of how their grief is supposed to look. Just because the death of a person we love has tossed our life into dysphoria does not mean the same is necessarily true for a child who is understanding, seeing, and thinking differently about the death than the adults in his or her life.

In the spring of 2012, I spoke with the eighth-grade student body of a school in central New Jersey. My task was to speak with them about expressing their feelings and honoring the diversity of their peers' feelings. My job was done almost as quickly as I had walked in the door. The students went to a school that taught about empathy. The kids, all by themselves, named and defined empathy and the ways in which they used it in their classroom. Context matters. Creating a healthy and safe community leads to increased resiliency. We create that space by talking openly about feelings, naming our needs, and providing children with tools to understand the human experience and our complex emotional selves.

The development of children is affected by the events in their lives and the context in which they learn about death, expressing their feelings, and the inner voices adults put in their heads. The boy who is told to be a man and not cry, the girl who is not allowed to play in the frog pond because it isn't ladylike, the child who is ignored because he does not meet his parent's expectations: each of these children will react to a death based on his or her context or upbringing.

The areas where we see dysfunction in a child's grief are seldom because of the grief itself. Self-destructive behaviors, verbal or physical confrontation with peers, and other unhealthy coping tools are often connected to dysfunction that existed in the child's life before the death. The grief simply provided a new and perhaps threatening context for it to play out in a different and uncontrolled way. Kids from a functional environment may still hit peers to express their frustration or feelings, but those who are unable to manage their own behavior and whose lashing out is ongoing may be expressing their grief in this way because of their context.

The need for a child to feel normal can be tremendous. Sometimes grieving kids work hard to change their context in order to preserve their normalcy. One of Good Grief's teenagers made a big decision when her mom died. Cathy's mom and dad divorced when she was eight, but she lived with her mom full time. Although Dad was incredibly active in her life, she didn't spend a lot of time at his house, especially since he lived some distance away, which made it difficult for Cathy to see her friends on the weekend.

When Cathy's mom came out of remission from her breast cancer, Cathy was at her side. She spent a lot of time with her mom and was well aware that her mom wasn't going to beat it this time. But, after Cathy's mom died, it became clear that she couldn't stay in the house by herself or attend the same school since it was so far from her dad's home and work. Cathy saw an opportunity and moved on it quickly. She realized that if she walked away from her school and her mom's house, moving in with her dad, she could keep her mom's death a secret. Cathy called up her friend, who attended the school Cathy would soon be attending, and sat her down. "Listen, I don't want people to know about my mom unless I decide to tell them. This is my story to share, not yours." Her friend complied.

Cathy didn't have to walk around town with everyone knowing who she was and that her mom had died. She could feel normal and not have to talk about it when she didn't want to talk about it.

One September, I spoke with the faculty of a middle school where a student had died over the summer and a teacher had died the year before. I asked the school social worker how the student's siblings were doing. She said that his brothers were confused because no one was talking about Jeff. Everyone ignored every conversation and reference to him. They weren't sure what to say and wanted to be sensitive, so they avoided any mention of Jeff. After my presentation, a line of teachers found me in the hall and had a lot of questions. They all had the deceased student's siblings in their classes. One was a biology teacher who wasn't sure how to juggle conversations about death, diseases, and dealing with dissections. One was an art teacher who wasn't sure how to facilitate a conversation around the kid's grief if it came up during an art project. Another was a Spanish teacher who was worried about the impact of teaching the traditional Mexican Day of the Dead holiday. Each of them eagerly wanted to do the right thing.

Luckily, these questions and conversations were happening in the first week of school and not months later. Many teachers and adults, in an attempt to be respectful, avoid anything that they suspect might arouse feelings or memories. But avoiding biology conversations about death, and not dissecting frogs, is an abnormality. Avoiding important and rich conversations about Mexican culture and how they honor their dead is an abnormality. Grieving kids want to be normal and treated as such. Often, supporting grieving children requires us to stay the course, but to do so with intentionality, open communication, and inclusivity. Rather than avoid all conversations on death or behave like it never happened, normalizing grief and offering support requires us to be in tune with kids through dialogue and attempting to understand their unique and individual needs.

While normalizing grief, it is important to normalize the many feelings that accompany grief. It's OK to be angry, numb, indifferent, relieved, uncertain, and in despair. It's OK to question or doubt God. As long as a child isn't doing anything unhealthy or destructive, we should not stop or get in the way of these feelings, because all of these reactions are normal. So many variables affect grief. The type of relationship we had with the person will influence our feelings. Not-so-nice people die, too. I have heard several children say, "I like my stepdad more than my real dad. He's nicer to me and he loves me." That's simply a reality for some kids. Similarly, the role that the deceased played in the life of the family and child will affect the grief. The implications of the sole provider dying have a unique impact, whereas the gender of the parent has an effect of its own. Each of these variables is a normal component of the process, provoking normal reactions. And whatever those thoughts and feelings are, most children simply want to feel and be treated like everyone else.

The objective is not to cross our fingers and hope grieving children will move out of town and start their lives all over, like Cathy's situation allowed. The goal is not to craftily orchestrate ways to avoid everyday conversations and topics that are important or relevant to learning and life. Instead, the hope is that everyday life and learning are done with intentionality and the awareness that these topics and conversations may be difficult for some. The caregiver's goal is an intentionality that pays attention to what kids are and aren't saying. It's listening. It's watching. It's acknowledging feelings or possible reactions when they are witnessed or highly likely. Normalizing grief is not finding ways to avoid it. Normalizing means engaging grief head-on with compassion, openness, and a willingness to learn and respond in the moment.

We cannot measure the success of how well we supported a grieving child. In fact, we may never know. However, we can know how well we listened, companioned, honored, and were present each step of the way. Although grief cannot be cured, each of us has the power to ensure that no child has to grieve alone.

Chapter 6

Listening without Lollipops

Silence Is Golden and Duct Tape Is Silver

Recently, a ten-year-old boy taught me a catchy phrase. It perfectly articulates the work of supporting the bereaved: "Silence is golden and duct tape is silver." I just love it! How often do we find ourselves in a room with someone who is being silent and simply present? I'm not a parenting expert, nor, frankly, am I convinced that anyone is. I think good parents are those who make decisions that are rooted in good values. My value system includes love, imagination, faith in love, learning, play, fun, commitment, and being in the moment.

As someone who works with grieving children, I can say that supporting a grieving child should be rooted in a holistic value system, by which I mean every child's emotional self should be honored and respected, especially in times of crisis and learning. I agree that there are times when adults know best and can predict what a child cannot. However, when it comes to grief, I have no reservations about saying that children usually know better than adults. Children are spontaneous, observant, in tune, inquisitive, flexible, vulnerable, and curious. These innate characteristics require a different parental response from the responses parents fall back on when wrestling with a child to do his or her homework. A grieving child uses and depends on these innate characteristics for survival and figuring out the world. These are superb qualities for coping.

And so when it comes to grief, we have to make a fundamental shift from all those hokey parenting books that insist parents are pack leaders and all-knowing sages that merely need to transmit their omniscience to unmanageable and delinquent children. At Good Grief, we have four basic rules that we all follow—kids and adults alike—so that the children can teach us how to support them. I share them because they are the essence of what we are talking about in this chapter.

Rule 1: Honor Diversity

Good Grief serves families from towns all over the central and northern part of New Jersey. New Jersey is a diverse place, filled with overflow from New York City and those looking for housing larger than a closet. As a result of this large geographical area, families from all walks of life receive support from Good Grief. We have the obvious diversity of race, sexual orientation, socioeconomic status, religion, and so on. But the diversity that the children are interested in is greater than the demographic boxes that we have become accustomed to placing check marks in on paperwork. For the children, diversity is far more than race or riches. The children understand diversity as the unique and different ways that we all grieve, remember, express ourselves, and try to understand death. For example, diversity at Good Grief can look like this: "Oh, your mommy is in heaven?" one girl says to another. "Well, I'm not sure where my mommy is. Daddy said heaven is for dreamers. I have a lot of dreams. By the way, what is a Lord and why does it have your mommy?" The differences in how they understand and interpret what adults have told them are met with respect.

Grieving children are in a very difficult position. They are surrounded by adults who believe—or at least act as if—they have all the answers. And if not that, many adults are uncomfortable with the "answers" they do have. Most children are given prescribed paths to "deal with" their grief. And many mental health professionals create that path with a treatment plan. What would it look like if we empowered the children or gave them an opportunity to find their own path? Well, that is much of what happens at Good Grief and at similar centers.

At centers like Good Grief, children are given an opportunity to explore their questions, express all their feelings, and simply be kids; hence the importance of honoring diversity. It's a rule with real, tangible meaning when ten kids approach the same subject in ten very different ways. And thus the magic: kids learning from kids. Together, in community, the children are able to talk about death and their feelings openly and often without hesitation. Those interactions are powerful only if everyone agrees to respect and understand one another. Such interactions are mostly reserved for peers because—to date—grieving children live in a society that alienates and misunderstands them.

Rule 2: No Interrupting

Grieving kids are pretty accustomed to being interrupted. "Aw, your mommy died. Well, you be strong for Daddy. You're the lady of the house now." Yikes! What does that mean? But, those interruptions and commands are what kids have to interact with every day. Most dialogue involves lecturing, adults questioning whether a child's tears are grief tears or manipulation, kids poking fun, and the silence of people avoiding the subject. What would it look like if adults just listened to kids explore their feelings, respecting the child's sharing and showing intent interest?

Rule 3: Only Give Advice If Asked

Here comes the shocker. Get ready. This may be hard to swallow: you do not have the answers. Your ideas may seem like good ideas, but there is a chance that what's a good idea for you is a bad idea or, in their words, a stupid idea for kids. The objective of supporting a grieving child is not to take away the pain. It is a willingness to be present in the midst of pain and uncertainty, exploration and play. Rather than, "Well, Ellen, you need to tell your mom that you feel she is dating the wrong man," try, "Ellen, next time your mom talks about him, what do you think you'd like to say to her?"

Rule 4: What We Say Here Stays Here

Just about everyone wants to feel safe when he or she is vulnerable. We want to know that we will not be judged and that what we share will not be used against us or used to punish us. We want to know that we will be met by support and love. And that is why confidentiality is so important. No one wants his or her story shared on the playground or at the diner. Kids want to know that they are respected and cared for at all times.

When a teenager shares in groups at Good Grief that he has gotten drunk, we do not run out of the room, tell his parent(s), and call a rehabilitation center. The fact of the matter is, a lot of teens get their hands on liquor and marijuana. If we give them the space to share what they are up to, then their peers can tell them that they are being reckless. We adults can hear what they are doing and determine whether it's unhealthy, and we can ask them if they find the said actions helpful. If we freak out and tell the teens how irresponsible, illegal, and shameful their actions are, then we will have accomplished only one thing: caressing our own naïveté.

Sure, we would not have to hear about it ever again and we could pretend that reality is different than it is, thus allowing us to uphold our belief that Sarah is a rule-following angel. But she's not. She is a teen exploring life. Instead, the safety of knowing that confidentiality will be upheld, unless she is hurting herself or others, provides a space for her to share, for her peers to test and confront her reasoning, and for us to gently inquire if this is the healthiest way to cope.

That's it: four basic rules to help our community follow the lead of grieving kids. Once we start to follow that lead, though, there are some skills we can develop to be more effective in supporting children as they do their grief work.

Talking to a Grieving Kid

I often tell people to throw away their grammar. Think in sentence fragments. If you are talking in paragraphs, then you are probably the only one hearing a word. There is no single best way to talk to a child. Remember, every child is unique and his or her needs are unique. The most important question I ask myself is, "Whom am I talking for?" Am I talking to feel important and share my thoughts, or to facilitate a conversation?

Of course, there are more and less effective ways of communicating. The reason so many adults stumble in communicating with their kids, especially with their teens, is because they lack some basic communication skills. "Joe, what did you learn in school today?" a mother asks, and naturally Joe responds with, "Nothing." "Joe, I want to know why you did this!" Mom exclaims, and naturally Joe hears the tone of his mother's voice and responds with, "I dunno."

To effectively communicate with kids, there are a few essential things to be mindful of: body, tone of voice, sentence construction, eyes, and self-awareness. What is my body doing? Do I look uncomfortable, relaxed, or indifferent? How about my voice? Is it inquisitive or ready for an inquisition? How do I express my sentiments, concerns, or interest, and does my voice mirror my desires? How is the tone of my voice communicating my feelings? Do I have good but not intimidating eye contact? Asking all of these questions of myself—being in tune with my body, communication, and desires—is part of my self-awareness.

Effective communication takes work. Often we are busy or get lazy, and as a result, our effectiveness quickly dwindles. But, if we are intentional about how we communicate, then we can be far more effective.

Open-Ended versus Closed-Ended Questions

I think the difference between open-ended and closed-ended communication is also linked to how we listen. Are we open to whatever a child might tell us, or are we hoping to direct it and receive only what we want to know? An open-ended question is very much susceptible to interpretation. So, while you thought you were asking about the day Mom died, the child chose to tell you about the hospital room and nurses. And that's incredibly effective. The child got to share what he or she wanted or needed to share, not what you hoped to learn.

An open-ended question—and sometimes it is more like a statement than a question—is constructed in a way that does not merit a yes or no answer: "I'm wondering what that day was like for you. Tell me about it." You could also say, "What was that day like for you?" Most kids are not going to say, "No," though they could say, "I don't know." And you might reply, "What have other people said about it?" The objective is not always to get a response, but rather to provide an invitation and an opportunity for sharing. The child who says "I dunno" may not be ready to share or confront scary feelings at that moment. So, that is not an invitation for you to practice constructing your open-ended questions until you get it right and can provoke a response. You are providing the opportunity to share in a safe way.

Reflective Listening

Most of my interactions with kids involve reflective listening: "Mr. Joe, my mommy died." And I reply, paying attention to my tone and nonverbal communication, "Oh, your mommy died." And then the child might say, "Yeah, she was sick." Reflective listening is a very helpful communication strategy. By mirroring or slightly repeating what you heard the child say, he or she knows you are paying attention. Especially with younger kids, they may only intend to throw out a few facts: she's dead, she was sick, I miss her, or I think she is in heaven. Many do not intend to give you a lengthy narrative, so reflective listening provides the space and the invitation for them to enter, control, and exit the conversation.

Forget the Lollipops

Much like the boys I mentioned in a previous chapter who needed encouragement to ride Kingda Ka, sometimes children need encouragement to talk about the person who died and their corresponding feelings. Sometimes, they need to know that you are a safe adult, you won't judge, you won't interrupt them, and that you care. We can tell the children all these things and remind them from time to time.

It is tempting for adults to be Pavlovian with children and introduce a reward system because we assume that talking about it is the most helpful thing for the child: every time the child talks about Mom he or she gets a lollipop or a trip to the toy store. But grief is more complex and complicated than toys and rewards. After all, we may think we are being helpful and supportive when we reward a child for talking about the dead and expressing his feelings, but that child has to go to school and function in a world that is not good about listening to or caring about his needs. If we push children to be vulnerable, perhaps before they are ready, or if we use incentives to lead them to believe it is always safe to share, I do not believe we are contributing to their development of healthy coping skills. Children are not dogs, and they deserve better than a treat system to learn about coping skills. Additionally, talking about it is not always helpful for every child. Part of a child's grief work is to develop her own lens for determining when it is safe to be vulnerable and when it may not be.

Instead, when a child chooses to share his or her story, in his or her own time, listen and affirm. Sometimes I say things like, "Other kids tell me that not everyone listens to them or that some people hurt their feelings. If that happens to you and you want to talk about Daddy, you can always talk with me." This also shows that I am a consistent presence, not one that shows up for the weekend or just visits a few times a year.

The true reward for sharing one's story and expressing one's feelings without interruption or judgment is knowing that people care and are interested. When faced with difficulties, the child will know that those same people will be there to help in the future. The development of healthy coping skills is a child being able to identify caring people, knowing she is loved, building relationships, and experiencing the therapeutic nature of community and friends. When a well-supported teen is faced with a problem, there is a stronger likelihood that he will choose good friends over booze to help him cope with losing the game or not getting into his dream college.

Communication is ultimately about building community and relationships, coping skills, and love. It requires patience, but the outcome is transformative. And to witness that transformation we must consistently be present.

The Power of Presence

Sometimes, when the situation is dire, showing up is the most compassionate thing we can do. In these moments, compassion looks like having the courage to drop everything, change course, and be present when you are not sure what else to do.

When John was dying in hospice, his teenage son Matt picked up the phone and called his church. Matt knew that his dad was dying and getting close to his last breaths. Sister Margaret rushed over to the hospice, even though she was not on call, and sat with Matt and John while Matt's mom and siblings were en route. Sister Margaret handed Matt some holy oil, and together they anointed Dad's head, heart, hands, and feet. Matt describes it as an incredible and holy moment in which he had the sacred role of blessing his dad moments before his dad died.

Sister Margaret changed course. She stopped tending to whatever her commitments were that day and became present to a family in need of support and caring presence. As a result of her spontaneity, her willingness to respond in the moment, and the generosity of her time, she gave Matt an opportunity to experience something sacred for him, his dad, and his family.

These moments are often missed because we decide to wait an extra day, collect more information, or get lost in our own busyness. But when we free ourselves of the excuses, we stumble into the sacred moments when a child shares a memory, a person departs from this earth, or the bereaved see in themselves the courage and hope to continue living and rebuilding their lives.

Being fully present to those who grieve is a sacred act. I do not use the word *sacred* loosely, especially since I know it is loaded with a lot of meaning for different people. However, the sacredness of presence is because there is a lack of absence, and I think absence is often rooted in apathy or fear. Being there for someone is an act of love, kindness, and generosity. It is sacred not only because it is needed, not only because those who have died cannot be present to comfort their loved ones, but also because we are increasingly unavailable to one another. Caring presence is sacred; it is special because it is rare. It is special because, at times, we are witnessing the breaking and rebuilding of someone's life, the reemergence of joy, the struggle of holding on and letting go, and the simple yin and yang that is entangled in everyday grief.

When we show up and listen, witness a child's story and follow her lead, and do so without the expectation of fixing her pain or getting anything in return, we are offering support. There may not be any incentives for supporting a grieving child, and at best we may know only that we care and that we extended compassion when it was needed most.

Chapter   7

On Death and Lying

When I worked at Connecticut Hospice, I spoke with
doctors from Yale-New Haven Hospital. They came on
tours of the facility and shadowed the hospice doctors on rounds
as they discussed the progression of a patient's disease, her comfort
level, palliative care, and support available to her and her family. I
always got nervous speaking to a cafeteria filled with doctors.

Here were a bunch of twenty-something students from a stu-
pendous hospital with some of the best doctors, listening to me talk
about "the good death" or the importance of holistic approaches
to medicine. I was friends with the hospice doctors and I grew up
surrounded by medical professionals, so I knew what these folks
were trained to do: save lives. Doctors function with a mentality
entrenched in diagnosis, treatment, and cures. Death, to a doctor,
is failure.

Luckily, Yale was training their doctors to be informed about
end-of-life care and the many variables that should be taken into
consideration when treating a terminal or potentially terminal disease. My conversations with these eager doctors were not combative,
which is not an unlikely scenario when one challenges the status quo
of something as important and self-important as medicine.

113

Doctors are trained to be fighters and saviors. For the majority of us, that's a pretty wonderful thing to have on our side when faced with illness. However, if medical professionals do not have a balanced and honest approach to medicine, then we have a real problem when faced with end-of-life decisions.

Currently, doctors function in a culture that has unrealistic expectations. We put a lot of our own fear of death on medical professionals, who may have a vast assortment of treatment strategies in their grasp but who are not, in fact, saviors, despite the treatment options. Many people expect doctors to do the impossible, and thus doctors are tempted to comply only to satiate the needs of someone who does not want to say good-bye to a loved one.

Often when I visited the bedside of a dying patient, the patient would deliver a long rant about the malpractices of his doctors, who were responsible for his impending death. When I first began this work, I was convinced that New Haven was run rampant with the world's worst doctors. From the patients' perspective, it sounded as though every doctor in the world had it out for them. It did not take me long to realize that the real issue was something deeper.

Now, juxtapose the patient's expectations of doctors with our culture surrounding the *C* word. Yes, now cancer is referred to as the "Big C." While medicine is making tremendous advances with cancer treatment, an increasingly pervasive mentality is distorting our relationship to cancer. Cancer is war. It's a battleground and a fight to the finish. We no longer die, but rather we lose our valiant battles against the disease. Some of us are winners while others of us our losers. We must fight! We must win!

In my line of work, that turns out to be a dangerous paradox. Many people are not given the opportunity to fight. Some people would make a different choice rather than spend months in the hospital only to live a few more months after that. However, we are creating a culture around how we are supposed to interact with and destroy cancer. Just to be clear, I hate and completely abhor cancer. I've seen what the disease, like many other diseases, does to individuals, families, communities, and children. However, I've also witnessed what our Big C culture is starting to do to how we think about treatment and its impact on families.

Let's cut to the chase: not all cancer should be treated, and not all lives can be saved. That's just a fact. We act as though all fights against cancer are honorable and noble, as if each cancer patient is dubbed a knight and sent forth from Camelot to war. One might wonder what the harm of trying is; at least it's an attempt to win, and a noble effort is better than the outcome of death. Well, we've made that assumption, a giant leap, without being informed about the pros and cons. The problem is that, in many instances, we may have forgotten the children.

Newly diagnosed patients depend on their support system, their doctors, and the hope that they'll be fine. The latter is what drives a willingness to take big risks and surrender the last days of one's life to the chance that the impossible becomes possible. The patient looks to his or her doctor and support system for direction. The doctor lays out the treatment plans and the support system usually says, "You can beat this; you'll be OK." And thus the medical journey begins in a millisecond, with little more direction than a pat on the back and some encouragement.

However, there is seldom an intermediary or advocate helping a scared and overwhelmed patient review the facts, reflect on his or her ideas about a good quality of life, and talk about ways to support the children through the process.

Currently, I perceive a lack of transparency around the fragility of life and the realistic expectations of various treatment plans. Rather than helping a patient understand the emotional and physical

115

costs of treatment, many medical professionals support patients in making uninformed decisions.

When Robyn was dying from breast cancer, she made a decision. At first, she had a mastectomy and underwent chemotherapy. As soon as she realized that her disease had metastasized, she changed course. Robyn could have continued with a lot of treatments, gone to the doctor and hospital on a weekly or daily basis, and fought as her friends encouraged her to do. However, she weighed her options. She sat with what I imagine must have been a flood of intense feelings and uncertainty. Robyn evaluated what "surviving" would have looked like and for how much longer she could have survived. She probably thought she might have a couple of years, maybe longer or shorter, if she got the cancer into remission.

Robyn decided that it was more important for her to be with her six- and nine-year-old boys at the time. She did not want to lug them to the doctors anymore. She did not want to be away from them during whatever time she had left. She looked into the face of uncertainty and made a decision. Instead of fighting and following the prescribed path, Robyn spent the last six months of her life visiting with friends and writing the kids notes for their sixteenth birthdays, graduations, wedding days, and other important events. She put together photo albums, and gave whatever love she had left to give. I think Robyn's story is an act of courage, and I imagine the decision was incredibly difficult. But just because a decision is hard or uncomfortable does not mean it is not a viable and really positive option.

I do not dare to suggest that Robyn's decision was the only right or healthy way to respond to her disease, as I do not know the details of her condition or her expectations of a quality life at the time. However, I think honestly facing a more-than-likely outcome is an important choice, and doctors, social workers, and chaplains need to communicate its pros and cons, especially while the status quo fighter mentality grows in universal acceptance.

How these decisions are made affects children. We need to imagine what a more thoughtful and intentional approach looks like before we can discuss how to support children during end-of-life care. I think it is pointless to think about how to support children in a broken system without evaluating the system itself.

I used to be confident that the problem lies in medical training, and therefore medical professionals. In many cases, I still am. But that doesn't mean that the solution has to come from the same pool of professionals. Perhaps we ask too much of doctors. Is it fair to ask them to work hard to save our lives and then also ask them to help us balance decisions about best next steps, treatments, and the most holistic approach to our medical care? Perhaps not.

Maybe our greatest allies are our own self-interest and advocates who can help distraught patients sort through the decisions. The point of the matter is, with these life-changing diagnoses, the uncertainty of illnesses that could send our lives into peril, we need to be surrounded by supportive people—whether they are doctors, chaplains, social workers, or other advocates—who are able to help us determine our ideal quality of life. But right now, most patients have to go at it alone and get caught up in the cogs that are the egos of medicine, the lack of resources, and the lack of knowledge.

We cannot control the uncertainty that children feel in times like these. We can't control their fear or their distress, either. However, we can maintain hope—not a false hope that it will all be OK, but the hope and knowledge that, although death may come, it will not destroy a child's life or the love that child is capable of giving and receiving. This is a shift in how we view and understand dying. In some cultures, the fears that we face in our context do not exist. Some see dying as a rebirth, a new life. They have an understanding or appreciation of death that does not look like our Western ideologies.

It is important to note these differences, not because other cultures are necessarily facing these realities better than we are, but to note that we have created these fears and ideas on our own, through our communal acceptance. So, in other words, it's completely up to us to decide how we want to see and interact with our mortality. Is death normal? Is it simply part of life? Is it a pillar of our human experience? Is it something horrid and worth avoiding at all costs? These questions are for us to decide.

Working with the dying and bereaved, I view death as a part of life and a natural variable in our human experience. Listen, I don't want to be faced with it anytime soon, certainly no more than anyone else. But how I view death is going to affect my dying if I am faced with a terminal illness. How do we, as individuals and a culture, view death and a good quality of life? In fact, how do we view life? What value systems do we build around our ideas about a good life? This is at the core of how we will view our dying and what we'll tell our children when that day comes.

Life and death are surrounded by choices. The problem is that we have come to fear death so much that we have lost track of all the choices we have regarding death and dying. Most people rarely talk about death. Most people don't think about, articulate, or explore with others what they think is a good quality of life. Our silence around this fundamental characteristic of our existence has left us uninformed and lacking in creativity. And now, when we are faced with our mortality, most people choose the fight because they think that's the only or best option.

One of the most transformative aspects of hospice is that it brings death into the home. Hospice professionals handle the majority of the patient's care and allow the spouse, parents, children, and friends to be present to the dying without fatigue from caregiving. As with any cultural shift, the hospice movement comes with its own institutional agendas, but the growth of hospice over the past thirty years has begun an important part of the cultural rebirth of how we care for our dying.

When Jason's dad was dying at home, Jason got to climb into bed with him, show him his artwork, and be the adoring five-year-old son his dad loved. Jason was there when his dad died. Mom asked him if he wanted to be in the room and Jason said "Yup" without hesitation. So, as a family, they all said good-bye, sang some of Jason's favorite songs to Dad, and grieved together.

When I met Jason he was a very quiet boy, not only in his interactions with me but also in his play. He wouldn't beat the drum, jump around, or talk loudly. He had spent the past three months being quiet so Daddy could rest. He had to change his behavior and press the pause button for a little bit so Daddy could be comfortable. Jason understood and respected why he had to behave differently, and his dad thanked him for it. With effective communication and support from his mom, Jason reclaimed his space in a short period of time, and toys and noise once again filled the rooms of their house after Daddy died.

Despite the many components—and I'd add sacrifices and challenges—of American culture shifting its practices regarding grief and death, there will be many great benefits. As a globalized society, we have made tremendous advances. Despite our progress, I don't believe we fully know yet what impact these changes will have on future generations.

How we handle end-of-life decisions are moral decisions in that they have impacts on individuals, families, and communities. Moreover, our medical and cultural practices affect how our children and future generations view disease and death; but most important, they affect how we understand a good quality of life. As much as reflecting on death may be about coping and making healthy decisions, it's equally about how we live. If we can't decide how we want to live our lives, we'll never determine how to let them go when the time comes.

Chapter 8

A Cultural Rebirth

Supporting grieving children is a cultural rebirth. It worries some people to think about it that way, but what else do we call a movement to return to a more holistic and natural approach to death and grief? What are we to call a reawakening, much like that started by Kübler-Ross in 1969, which begs us to stop, communicate, acknowledge, and transform the structures that are negatively affecting our entire culture, especially our children? It sounds like a rebirth to me.

I'm not sure how it could be anything else. If we are to stop or take a break from our busy lives and be available to our peers and those in need of support, we must recoil against the temptation to avoid difficult conversations and hard realities. If we are to return to a sense of community where physical presence is more important than virtual presence, we need to revolt against the distances we've built between our human relationships and physical contact, giving life to a new way of being. If we are to do any of the things I propose, we need organizations to support us, and that requires a culture that demands it. A community of understanding adults and professionals, educated and competent about grief, looks very different from the uncomprehending and uninformed adults that currently confront our grieving children.

It's a rebirth with many parts, including medicine, funeral rituals, support of the bereaved, and how we honestly communicate diagnoses. It involves the living and the dead.

With that said, I confess I am probably the worst dinner guest of all time. Well, that's not entirely true. I am only terrible if people hound me about my profession and show too much interest. Luckily for most people, I don't bring it up unless asked, since I like to take a break from death talk from time to time, myself. The part of this conversation that makes me hard to be around is my refusal to talk about this cultural rebirth without talking about the dead. I don't believe we can fully discuss children's bereavement if we don't discuss our culture's hang-ups with dead bodies.

In 2005, Sal, a Sicilian immigrant, died at hospice while I was his chaplain. Naturally, he and I had had a lot to talk about, since anything involving Sicily catches my attention. I was present when he died. His death was a bit of an ordeal for his family, because only one of his sons was present when Sal unexpectedly had a heart attack in his hospice bed. I was asked to be present when Sal's wife and grandkids arrived at the hospice. His son called them at home and decided not to tell them on the phone about the death, so I was present when they arrived and the news was shared. Sal's son took the family to the chapel to convey the news of Sal's death.

After receiving the news, the family went to the bedside and spent some time with Grandpa. I was present when he was washed and moved to a room, which we called the "holding room," to wait for the funeral home to come get him. The family had left, but about thirty minutes later they returned because Sal's young grandson, probably eleven- or twelve-years-old, wanted Grandpa's watch, which was still around his wrist.

Standing at the nurses' station, I overheard the conversation among the nurses, who were scared to take the watch off of a dead man's wrist. Naturally, I was befuddled since I had watched them clean and prepare Sal for his family only a short time beforehand. However, they were completely uncomfortable. So, I went to the holding room, lifted Grandpa's arm, and removed the watch. When I came up the elevator, I was met by Sal's son, who looked me in the eye and said, "I want to be like you when I grow up." He was moved by the simplest of gestures that, for a moment, he thought his son would be denied. His response to me demonstrated how important this act was for him, even though it felt to me simply like the appropriate thing to do.

I did not view Sal as a zombie or some scary manifestation of a former self. He was a person who had died and whose body needed care and respect. Yet, so many people are afraid of the dead, even those who have to interact with them. In the same light, I think it is interesting that many funeral directors do not handle the dead directly. They leave the embalming process and transportation of the dead up to embalmers. I've heard some funeral directors describe working with the dead as "icky," which seems so foreign to me, especially since one funeral director told me, "A dead body is less dangerous than a living one because it can't breathe. The dead can't spread pathogens!" So, what's the fear? Yet, the dead are shuffled out of sight, managed by strangers who orchestrate their care and disposition, and their deadness is fairly inaccessible to, say, a child. This fact only reinforces the need for a cultural rebirth.

We've created a system called the funeral industry to do what is inconvenient for us, or what we are not interested in doing. However, this system comes with very big consequences. For example, have you ever heard of a nonprofit funeral home? And do you think anyone would donate to it? My issues with the industry are not simply rooted in the high cost of a funeral. We created that system out of our expectations, so that cost, in part, is our own doing. Unfortunately, this system has a huge impact on the poor, who need to bury their dead also. The impact of the funeral industry on our rituals, our grief, and our children is worrisome and calls for reform.

Not every family has the opportunity to interact with the person who has died. Some people's bodies aren't returned to their families, and some don't return looking like their former selves because of how they died. But for those of us who are privileged to have the opportunity—the choice—to care for and interact with those who have died, as many families do at hospice, we get to touch, see, comprehend, and interact with our loved one. As someone who has witnessed thousands of families support their dying family members and care for them day in and day out at hospice, I see a major disconnect between that compassionate care and our current mortuary rituals.

Adults may react to this sentiment with extreme reservation or disgust, which is expected since most of us have been taught to fear the dead. In reality, though, most people's experience with the dead is limited or nonexistent. So really, we fear what we don't know. Unfortunately, that fear is transmitted to our children, who could benefit from more thoughtful and intentional rituals that attempt to meet their needs, including a natural curiosity about the unknown.

When the day comes when we get over our hang-ups about dead bodies, a child will approach those interactions with Mom or Dad or Grandpa with the same curiosity and need to learn as he would when he uses a stick to poke a dead cat in the backyard: "Guys, check out this cat. It's totally dead. Stiff as a board. Wow! Look at that!" That's not gross. That's learning. Children are tactile and need these interactions to gain knowledge for understanding.

Each of us, in our own way, tries to understand what it means to be dead. What does it mean to be embodied? What happens to Dad when he transitions from hugging and loving us to looking so different from his living self? What does it mean to look so alive and then look so dead? How will that affect my future relationship with him, as I process his death and rebuild my life without his presence? These questions are part of our meaning making.

Entrenched in our understanding of death are questions about our living and dying. How do we want to live knowing, truly knowing, that we will die? Do you want to be the person who has the well-decorated cubicle at your sixty-hour-a-week job, or the caring person who was present for those you loved most? These are questions about morality and value systems. And ultimately, they are questions about what type of adults we want our children to become. Do we want our children to develop healthy coping skills as the result of a supportive community, or do we want them to meander through a world with many realities that go undiscussed and hidden until our children are forced to deal with them?

These questions do not function in isolation. These decisions and this discussion may not affect your child, but they will affect the bereaved child who experiences the death of his mother. He is the child whose friends are nowhere to be found because the silences and stigmas we have created exacerbate the obstacles of grief all the more. It may be your child who isn't there for a friend, because you haven't modeled what it means to be a caring and competent friend to the bereaved.

The beauty of our American grief is that there is actually a lot we can control. We cannot control when our loved ones die or the complexity of our feelings. However, as a culture and community, we have within our grasp the ability to break down the isolation and unhealthy coping that we have inherited and helped to create. We simply have to agree to make the change. That part is completely up to us. In fact, the onus is entirely on us for future generations.

We've seen the impact our culture has had on children over the past 150 years, creating isolation and incompetence around children's grief. We can shift gears and get on track to a healthier culture right now, but we have to be willing to make major adjustments to a status quo that has enabled the dysfunction that has become our American way of grieving.

In this regard, the work of a cultural rebirth—the work of supporting grieving children—is dependent on us changing how we prepare for death, handle our dead, and support our bereaved. It's all interconnected—from doctors honestly disclosing terminal illnesses, to parents honestly talking about death with children, to us all changing how we mourn and remember.

What we tell the children is dependent on how willing we are to change, evolve, show up, and live in this world. What we end up telling the children will be determined by our presence or absence, our ability to choose love instead of clichés, and our courage to have faith in each child's ability to build a life never imagined.

In the meantime, many grieving moms and dads will have to continue taking risks and showing extraordinary courage to get help for their families, just like Teri did. Every day, until Teri found Good Grief, she combed the obituaries. She had her eyes on two things: the age of the deceased and his or her survivors. Anyone her age or who had kids the same ages as her kids was highlighted. Teri researched the families and located each of them.

A few weeks after the funeral, Teri would show up at their house with a rose and introduce herself, sharing that she and her girls understood how uncertain life could feel after the death of a loved one. After expressing her sympathy and support, she followed up and tried to build relationships, connecting with people so that she and her children were not alone in their grief. Out of desperation, Teri did her research, bought roses, and went in search of support and hope.

My hope is that the day will come when no one has to seek support because, as a community, we will have arrived at a time when support is all around, without question or doubt, and forever present in all that we do, especially in the lives of children.

Notes

3. Myths

1. *Diagnostic and Statistical Manual of Mental Disorders*, 4th ed., text revision (Washington, DC: American Psychiatric Association, 2000).

4. Components of a Child's Grief

1. Madelyn Kelly and Phyllis Silverman, *A Parent's Guide to Raising Grieving Children: Rebuilding Your Family after the Death of a Loved One* (New York: Oxford University Press, 2009).

2. J. William Worden, *Children and Grief: When a Parent Dies* (New York: Guilford Press, 1996).

CPSIA information can be obtained
at www.ICGtesting.com
Printed in the USA
FSHW04n2339160418
47009FS